# THE SIX STEPS TO
LASTING WEALTH

THE SIX STEPS TO LASTING WEALTH

TRANSFORM YOUR MINDSET, FINANCES, HEALTH, AND HAPPINESS

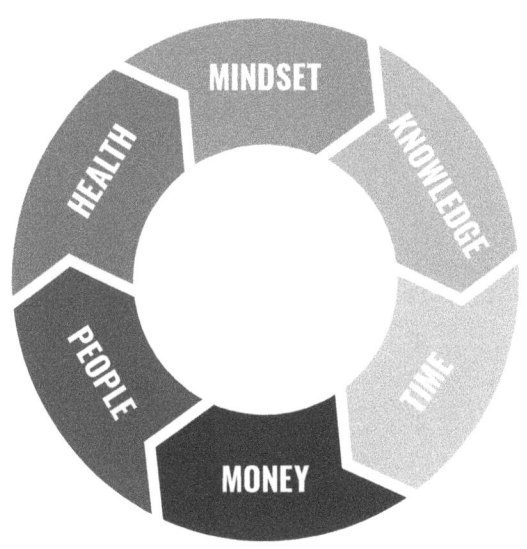

JOSEPH HERBERT

Copyrighted Material

The Six Steps to Lasting Wealth
Transform Your Mindset, Finances, Health, and Happiness

by Joseph Herbert & www.SelfMadeWealth.co

Copyright © 2024 by Joseph Herbert. All Rights Reserved.

All rights reserved. No part of this publication may be reproduced, distributed, or transmitted in any form or by any means, including photocopying, recording, or other electronic or mechanical methods, without the prior written permission of the author, except in the case of brief quotations embodied in critical reviews and certain other noncommercial uses permitted by copyright law. For permission requests, send communications to the author, listed below.

For information about this title, contact the publisher:

Joseph Herbert
www.SelfMadeWealth.co
Joe@SelfMadeWealth.co

ISBNs:
978-1-7341332-3-3 (hardcover)
978-1-7341332-4-0 (softcover)
978-1-7341332-5-7 (eBook)

Library of Congress Control Number: 2019918467

City of Publication: Erie, PA

First Printing edition 2020
Second Printing edition 2024

Cover and Interior design: 1106 Design

This book is dedicated to any person who wants to learn how to take control of their life, transform their thinking, get clear on what they want from the universe, and take bold action to make their dream come true.

ACKNOWLEDGMENTS

To *my parents for never giving up on me*. I know I made your life very difficult at times. Thank you for always telling me I could do better. Thank you for being so selfless and working hard all your lives, so that my brother, sisters, and I could have a better life. I have your incredible work ethic. I will never forget what you did for me. My mother always told me to "Never settle for anything in life." I never forgot she said that.

Thank you to my wife for all her support and faith in me to succeed. Thank you to Molly, Flower, and Edy for always going crazy when I get home. It is the best feeling in the world.

I am so thankful for all the great families who lived on 21st Street when I was growing up. All of you had a great positive influence on me. Every day that goes by, I realize how critical you all were to my success.

I want to thank my first business partners for getting me involved in real-estate investing. Thank you to all my Mastermind friends for allowing me to "never be the smartest person in the room."

I am saving the best for last. Thank you to my Lord for giving me such a blessed life and allowing me to be in a place where I can help other people have a better life.

◆ ◆ ◆

TABLE OF CONTENTS

Preface xi
Introduction xxiii

LIFE ASSET #1
   Mindset 1

LIFE ASSET #2
   People 39

LIFE ASSET #3
   Time 67

LIFE ASSET #4
   Knowledge 89

LIFE ASSET #5
   Money 99

LIFE ASSET #6
   Health 119

Final Thoughts 133
About the Author 137

PREFACE

The people who typically inspire authors to write books are usually close to the author, like a parent, spouse, or child. Sometimes, it is a mentor, business partner, or a close friend. My inspiration comes from a completely different group of people: all the people out there whom I have never met and who are struggling every day just to maintain what they have in life.

These people (maybe this is even you right now) are my inspiration because my own life story relates. It starts with my family. First, let me say I love and respect my mother and father very much. My parents are two of the most selfless people I know. They both had incredible work ethics. My siblings and I were truly blessed to have them as our parents, and I would not change that for anything. My father was my fishing and sports-watching buddy. When I was growing up, he never put his personal needs before the needs of his family. My mother was extremely hardworking and the most giving person I have ever met. She was an angel. I want to say this because, going forward in this book, I might seem disrespectful toward my parents with some of my perspectives and stories. I respect my parents, but I need to tell the truth about my family background to communicate the enormous effect the knowledge in this book has had on my life.

My father was a person who worked diligently throughout his life. For most of my youth, he had two jobs to make ends meet. He did not finish high school and never had anyone in his life to help him with money, business, or a positive mindset. No matter what went wrong with my father's life, it was instantly someone else's fault. I watched my father make one bad personal and business decision after the next. His life never changed financially or socially.

My father spent 20 or so years working at a grocery store as a butcher and produce-department manager. Two years before he was eligible for a full pension, he left his job at the grocery store to go into business for himself, opening a fishing-tackle store. Unfortunately, he paid thousands of dollars for inventory that was obsolete.

Eventually, my father failed in the fishing-store venture and had to close his doors. Shortly after the store closure, the sheriff showed up at our house to post a foreclosure notice. My mother, fortunately, knew the sheriff and persuaded him to come back in a few weeks. He never returned, so I can only guess my mother borrowed some money from her siblings and caught up on the mortgage.

My mother worked in the same shoe store for minimum wage for more than 40 years. It was the only job she ever had. She always put that store before her personal life and made countless sacrifices with her time and income so that the shoe store could succeed. I remember when she had her 25-year anniversary as an employee—the owner came over to our house and gave her a gift of a new watch. My mother cried when she opened the gift, weeping like a person who had just hit the lottery. I couldn't believe my mother thought a $50 watch was a great reward for 25 years of personal sacrifice, running this man's shoe store for him. After she received the watch, my mother worked another 15 years for the same employer. After 40 years in the same job, she had no ownership interest, no stock options, no 401(k), and no pension.

PREFACE

Belief systems and perspectives are inherited from our environment and mostly from our parents. My parents did not have the mindset, belief systems, or knowledge of people with personal or financial freedom. As I grew up, neither did I. I had turned out just like my father when it came to problem-solving, conflict resolution, and building relationships. I would blame everyone else but myself for what happened to me. I did not stick with anything I started. I was great at criticizing others. I was sent home from grade school at least once a week for bad behavior. I was almost held back in high school, and I flunked out of college after one year. I could go on for several pages about all the foolish mistakes I made, but I think you get the picture. My life was lived in the moment, without a single thought about even the second half of the day I was in.

But, my life changed. Throughout this book, you will read stories about how I did that. I went from virtually nothing to a life of personal and financial freedom. You will read about how I changed from failing to succeeding in ways that nobody could have predicted. Since I am living proof, I want everyone to have the tools to do the same.

Living Life by Default, or on Purpose?

You don't have any choice about who your parents, siblings, or relatives are. You're stuck with them because that's what you're born into. Generally, your first friendship happens like this: You walk outside. Some little kid next door walks outside, and you're both like, "Oh, let's be friends." Right? He could wind up being a serial killer, but you don't know. We live next door to each other. I don't have a car. I'm five years old. And then your parents tell you not to talk to strangers. So, you really don't try to make any new friends. Then you go to school, and the kids sitting around you become your friends. Then you get your first job, and your co-workers become your friends.

Up to the age of eighteen or twenty, almost every person in our life is there by default. Even later than that, most people never think about identifying the type of people they want to be around and then trying to find those people. I didn't—I went into business partnership with the best friends that I grew up with. They were not bad or dishonest people, but we had different business styles. I could never try to run the business the way it should have been run. I didn't figure it out until after that business marriage that we weren't good business partners.

All of this struck a chord in me, and I made a note of it.

After high school, when my friend decided to go to medical school, I went to school for earth science. I flunked out in a year and a half. I had a 0.6 cumulative GPA, and I was getting all kinds of letters from the school saying that if I didn't get my grades up, they were going to get rid of me. So, I quit. My parents flipped out, and I went and got a job.

I worked in construction for two years, and it was back-breaking. I was literally digging ditches and pushing wheelbarrows full of mortar. Then I saw this big ad in the paper about how we're going to have a technology boom, and we're going to need thousands of engineers. Simply because there was a need for that, I said, "I think I'll go back to college and be an engineer. It looks like I could get a job." It wasn't something I loved. It wasn't something my parents did. I didn't have an interest in learning about electrical and mechanical engineering.

But I went back. I got serious. I got my degree, and I got a job in engineering. I didn't *hate* it—I just *never liked* it. It wasn't a good fit for my personality. I heard a very wealthy business entrepreneur instructing someone to figure out what they want to do, saying, "If you don't love what you're doing, get out of it right away. Go find what you really want to do."

I realized I'd never really thought, even for one second, about what I wanted to do in life. And I had two parents who always said,

"You're going to go to school; you're going to get a job." They never said, "What do you think you want to do with your life?" I was living my life by default—there were no conscious decisions structuring my life.

I began making notes of all these things and putting a lot of thought into them.

Figuring It Out

By the time I was forty-five, everything seemed to hit rock bottom. My businesses were on the brink of failure, and so were my business partnerships. I had just ended a long-term romantic relationship, which was emotionally devastating. I lost my condo, and I was living in an old, run-down apartment. I was financially drained and despised my job. To top it all off, I went through a business divorce. The culmination of all this stress landed me in the hospital for five days.

I initially rushed myself to the emergency room, thinking I had appendicitis. It turned out my colon was severely inflamed due to stress and colitis. The doctors even suggested removing my colon, emphasizing how dire my condition was. Despite their recommendations, I decided against it. Deep down, I knew that external factors—my excessive drinking, poor diet, and the immense stress from my job and failing business—were the root cause.

When I was finally discharged from the hospital, I weighed a mere 122 pounds. During my hospital stay, I had to walk the hallways, pushing the stand that held my IV bags, just to get some movement after spending days confined to a bed. I looked so gaunt and unhealthy that a friend who came to visit his father at the hospital saw me and thought I was terminally ill. "Hey dude, do you have cancer or something?" he asked. He assumed I had either cancer or AIDS, given how terrible I looked. That was a wake-up call for me.

After leaving the hospital, I stumbled upon the reality show, *The Apprentice*. Now, whether you like Donald Trump or not, I have to mention him because this was the year his show debuted. It was a revelation for me. It was the season where they brought on young professionals to compete for a one-year apprenticeship with him. During the show, they would have these little sidebars where Trump would talk about surrounding yourself with the right people, focusing only on doing what you love, and having a positive attitude. I never thought about that stuff, but his words resonated with me. He talked about surrounding yourself with winners and positive people, and I thought to myself, *Here I am, 45 years old, and I never once in my life considered who I was spending time with.*

Around six months after my hospital stay, I think I actually had mild depression. I lost the condo that I was living in. I didn't get foreclosed on, but I had to sell it. I couldn't afford the payment. I had no money. I lost every asset that I owned in the business divorce. I had $30,000 in credit-card debt, I was super sick, and I looked terrible. I had a horrible mentality.

The Right Person at the Right Time

I had just gotten my real-estate license, and I was selling real estate part-time while still working in the technology field. My friend, a fellow agent, said to me, "I'm going to give you a CD of something I want you to listen to, because you're super negative. You just gotta change your attitude."

I remember driving to Pittsburgh to see my sisters and listening to the CD called *The Strangest Secret,* by Earl Nightingale. (As of this writing, you can find it for free all over the Internet.) The CD ran for about 90 minutes. I was anxious to get to this "secret" that Nightingale was talking about. I wanted, I *needed*, something to change. I was able to listen to it in its entirety on the way to Pittsburgh. Nightingale finally gets to the punchline, and what's the strangest secret? **We become what we think about.**

That shattered the prison cell I was living in. Just shattered it. I realized I had become the sum of all of my thoughts: everything that I saw through my lens, the people I was surrounding myself with, what I was doing, what I was not doing. This just blew me away.

I couldn't believe it. All the anecdotes and examples in that CD seemed to be aimed directly at me. On the way back home, I listened to it again. I probably listened ten or fifteen times. I remember getting home and just processing all I'd heard and thinking about all these things I had done and was doing wrong in my life.

An Epiphany

For at least five or six years, I kept writing down these examples in my life of what I'd done wrong and what I could have done differently. I had failed my way through much of my life. I didn't have any mentors. I didn't have any coaches. I love my father, God rest his soul, but I inherited the victim mentality from him, and it doesn't have to be that way.

The epiphany began with ten key things that I called the Principles of Success, and, like many great ideas—it happened in the shower. As I pondered all the things I'd done wrong and could have done differently, and what I could change after my new knowledge, I came up with these ten things. I literally turned off the shower, wrapped a towel around me, ran to my computer, opened up a Word document, and began to list these ten principles.

Over time I started grouping mistakes, ideas, and concepts together and began to see some common threads. Many of these stories had to do with people. Many had to deal with health. Some were about money, knowledge, or how I used my time. In this logical grouping, the Ten Life Principles became **the Six Life Assets: Mindset, People, Time,**

Knowledge, Money, and Health. If things are going wrong (or right!) in any area of your life, you can browse through this list, and you can see how it is most certainly directly related to one of these assets.

Your Assets

My life was already changing dramatically at this point, for the better. My real-estate career was taking off. I was making a lot of great new friends again. I joined our local Rotary Club. I became a full-time real-estate agent, and it was *so freeing* to get out of the corporate world! I gave up something that I thought I should be doing but didn't love.

That's when I realized these ideas I was writing down were really assets. If you understand them and use them correctly, they will take you anywhere you want in life. And for almost every person I meet who's unhappy, I could sit down and interview them, and find out how they have let these things become liabilities—or how other people around them have turned them into liabilities.

I'm a big believer in the Law of Attraction. However, when I hear people mention it, usually they frame it incorrectly, as if, in order to get the good things in life, you must get the Law of Attraction working for you. In reality, the Law of Attraction is always working. If your life isn't satisfying, the Law of Attraction is working—it's just bringing bad things into your life. It's not the Law of Positive Attraction, right? It's the Law of Attraction. I believe in that. I believe in the laws of the universe.

But the next level above that metaphysical world is the tangible world. That's where the Six Life Assets live, and that's what I love about them. They're not magic. You don't have to spend any money. You already have them all in your life. You're either squandering them and making them liabilities, or you're using them to get what you want out of life. But they're there. They are in every person's life. You already have everything you need.

PREFACE

You don't have to go to college. You don't have to go out and buy the kit. These already exist in your life. You only need to find out what these things are, assess what you're currently doing with them, and then figure out how to do the best things possible with them. Because when you do that, I can tell you: Everything in your life will change. And if you don't do it, probably nothing in your life will change.

Use the information in this book to decide your answer to this question:

If you are exactly the same five years from now, will you be okay with that?

I wrote this book because so many people today are stuck in a life of financial misery. Being mired in debt and barely making ends meet is a life of stress and worry. Today most people do not possess the beliefs, decisions, mindset, goals, daily habits, and environment that allow them to think, act, and live like a rich person and enjoy financial freedom. This mindset is not taught in any school. A bigger problem is that most people do not understand what it takes to change their lives to acquire these skills and tools. Without a book like this or professional help, most people will not be able to identify and understand the social, emotional, educational, and financial barriers that are holding them back or how to remove these barriers.

It is impossible to change your financial situation without changing most other aspects of your life. Changing your life must come first if you want to change your net worth and income. It is not the other way around. You don't become wealthy and rich first and then decide to make some changes. The only time the money comes before change is if you win a hefty sum, you inherit the money, or you steal it. I guarantee your life will not change if you acquire money by these methods. Because your mindset has not changed first, you will not like what happens afterward. You won't have the money for very long, and you may suffer other consequences.

Reading This Book

So why should you read my book? What makes me the right person to write a book like this? If a person like me figured out how to learn from my mistakes, realized there is a better way to live my life, found that better way, and greatly prospered from it personally and financially, you might want to listen up.

If you have never been face down in a mud puddle, completely broke, and questioning yourself and who your friends are, then you shouldn't be giving advice to people who are in that situation. I have been in that mud puddle. I've been poor and broke. I've made lots of money and lost it. I spent time doubting myself, analyzing my past, blaming everyone else except myself, and dwelling on my regrets. To sum it up, I have been there, I know what it is like, and I know how to change it.

Today I own a successful real-estate brokerage, numerous cash-flow-producing rental properties and motels, and an online education company. I am a self-published author. I enjoy numerous vacations every year. Today, on a scale of one to ten, I would rate my life a ten, and it is getting better every day. I believe the turnaround in my happiness, health, love life, wealth, and future growth has been nothing short of miraculous.

The simple fact that I started with nothing, made every mistake in the book, was completely unaware of how I was making decisions, and still figured out how to turn it around and build and live a better life, makes me the perfect person to write this book. If I can turn my life around and be successful, then you can, too.

The good news is I am here with this book to help you learn from both my mistakes and my successes so you don't have to go through

PREFACE

what I went through. Trial and error and learning the hard way are not good paths to success and becoming rich. My biggest motivation for writing this book was the many times I wished someone had shared a book like this with me while I was struggling to succeed in life. I owe it to the universe to put this book together for people like you so that you can enjoy the incredible life I am enjoying.

It is human nature to want to share something spectacular that has happened to you. Think about the following scenarios. When fishermen catch a trophy fish, they can't wait to tell their fishing buddies. When you hit a hole-in-one in golf, you call your friends immediately and share every detail of how it happened. When you hit the lottery, you run home and tell your spouse.

When I had my "epiphany" and realized how to start living with personal and financial freedom, it was like hitting the lottery. The day I started studying these principles and beliefs and applying them to my own life, my enthusiasm to change my life for the better was all I could think about, and my attitude shot through the roof. I had won a lottery more valuable than any money lottery: a priceless lifetime gift of exploring and achieving everything life offers. My happiness, love life, wealth, and health have been increasing and improving ever since this discovery.

Ever since my life has changed so dramatically for the better, it has become very important to me that I am given the chance to help people like you change your life for the better. I am totally committed to helping you achieve your maximum potential and obtain and maintain success in all areas of your life. Please give me your trust and focus, and I promise to start you down the path of self-discovery and enjoyment of all that life offers. I will do everything in my power to help you make your life better.

♦ ♦ ♦

INTRODUCTION

FINDING PERSONAL AND FINANCIAL FREEDOM

We *often hear about the poverty mindset*, scarcity mindset, or victim mentality. I grew up with all of these, and if you view life through this lens, you're setting yourself up for disaster. This book is really about my transition from that limiting perspective to a more empowering one focused on financial abundance and personal freedom. I just want to give this information to anybody who wants it. I don't want anyone to go through life like I did—always learning the hard way.

I've studied how to grow—whether educationally, financially, or in terms of investments. I even managed to get a college degree and ran a business for a while. Despite those experiences, I've faced failure in nearly every other aspect of my life. My romantic relationships didn't work out, I was a poor student, and I hopped from job to job. I also lost many friends along the way. No matter what happened, my immediate reaction was to find someone else to blame. I never took responsibility for my own actions or circumstances. I wanted something more. Like most people, I thought that if I could just be rich or wealthy, my problems would be solved.

What does it actually mean to be "rich"? If you ask a hundred people what their definition of "wealth" is, you will get a hundred different answers. Most of the answers will contain statements about acquiring a large amount of money, owning a big house, buying a luxury car, partying on a yacht, or not having to work anymore. The more I've analyzed my own journey, **I've realized that true wealth or "being rich" is purely about personal and financial freedom.**

I want to be very clear about three critical premises you must understand and believe if you are going to become personally and financially free:

1. Personal and financial freedom has absolutely nothing to do with the amount of money a person has or receives, or if they own expensive things.

2. Only working smart and hard over time and bringing value to other people will change the amount of money a person regularly earns and keeps.

3. If you want to become personally and financially free and stay there, you must learn how to leverage your **Six Life Assets: Mindset, People, Time, Knowledge, Money, and Health.**

INTRODUCTION

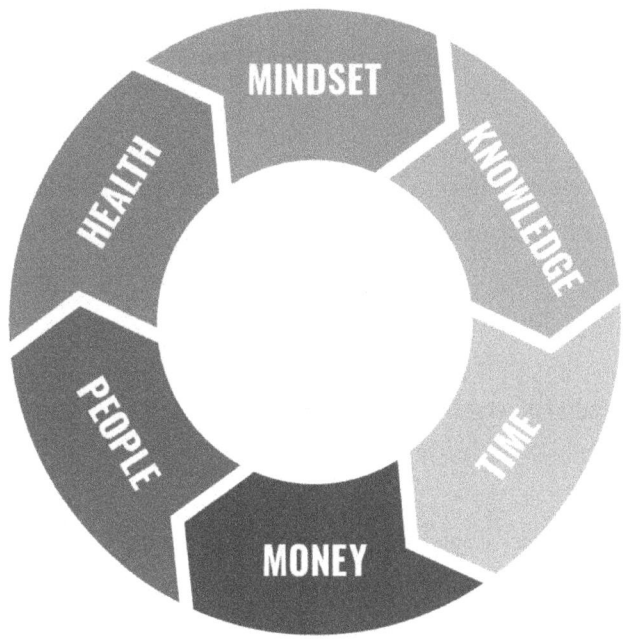

PREMISE 1

Think about the first premise. More often than not, when people talk about building wealth and being rich, it revolves around money. But "being rich" is so much more than money and what money can buy. The true meaning of *being rich* is defined by a person's quality of life, not by amounts of money or luxury possessions. Zig Ziglar often spoke of success in these terms: "People want to be happy, healthy, reasonably prosperous, and secure; they want to have friends, peace of mind, good family relationships and hope." Based on this view of being rich, you probably want to stop reading this book. As Tom Cruise said in the movie *Jerry Maguire*, "Show me the money!" You probably want me to show you the money right now, not the quality of life.

During my journey to alter my mindset, habits, decisions, income, and net worth, I became aware of these two facts:

- If I were to give most people a large sum of money, an expensive home, and a luxury car, it would not change their lives, and they would not be rich.

- If a person reads this book and applies the knowledge, beliefs, wisdom, and mindset in the following pages, that person will have the greatest chance of changing their life and living with personal and financial freedom.

Please read the statement below several times. This is another basic concept you must understand.

> *"Rich people don't live their lives the way they do because they have a lot of money. Rich people have a lot of money because of the way they live their lives."*

When most of society views people who are personally and financially free, enjoying the best things in life, they assume that is the benefit of having a lot of money. Rich people know that the money they have in their possession does not truly belong to them. Because of the way they think, act, speak, and bring value to other people, the world has allowed rich people to control large sums of money. Wealthy people use this money to enrich their own lives and empower themselves to help other people. That is why rich people don't focus on the amount of money they control. People who are personally and financially free have confidence knowing that, if they take care of money and use it to help other people, their own lives will be enriched. They know more money will flow to them every day.

You can help a person cross the street or let a person get in line in front of you. I highly encourage you to do these types of courteous and gracious gestures every day, whenever the chance presents itself.

INTRODUCTION

The world needs a lot more of this type of courtesy. Being nice to other people is also good for your immune system and emotional outlook on life. These things make you wealthy.

When you are personally and financially free, you can help people on a much larger scale than just holding the door for them. You can use your money to open a school to teach underprivileged children about investing and entrepreneurial skills. You can donate money to a non-profit organization that helps homeless people. You can open a soup kitchen for hungry people. You can give tuition scholarships to underprivileged children to help pay for their post-high-school education. Doing small favors is nice, and we need more of it, but a rich person with money can have a deeper, more impactful, and longer-lasting effect on people. Being rich is less about the simple fact of the money and more about how it is used and how you give back.

Below is a list of the qualities and traits of a person living personally and financially free. Whenever I talk about a rich person, a wealth-building person, from this point forward, I am talking about a person who:

- is honest and ethical.

- respects and loves themselves and the people they surround themselves with.

- is well-liked by their friends, family, clients, employees, and customers.

- values their health and lives a healthy lifestyle.

- shows up on time and does what they say they are going to do.

- holds themselves accountable for their actions and the outcome of their efforts.

- works smart and hard over time to build their wealth and passive income.

- uses their services and products to bring value to other people.

- charges a fair price for their goods and services.

- owns assets like rental property, stocks, mutual funds, and businesses.

- avoids bad debt.

- works on things they are passionate about.

- knows their strengths and weaknesses.

- knows how to use leverage.

- can quit their day job because their investments provide enough passive income to support their standard of living and allow them to continue to acquire additional investments.

- constantly pursues change and personal growth by reading, watching, and listening to positive educational content.

- always networks with other prosperous people.

- is constantly looking for their next mentor or coach.

- attends seminars and conferences to learn more about investing.

- acquires new skills, expands their field of expertise, or learns about a new discipline they are interested in pursuing.

Notice that, in this list, there is no mention of a large amount of money, an expensive house, luxury cars, or a big boat. Again, I want to

INTRODUCTION

reinforce the premise that being rich has absolutely nothing to do with the amount of money a person has.

Large sums of money are acquired and lost all the time. Living like the person described in the list above will allow you to consistently acquire and keep money, treat it with care, and do meaningful things with it.

PREMISE 2

A second concept I repeatedly refer to in this book is that only working smart and hard over time to bring value to other people will change the amount of money a person regularly earns and keeps. This version of personal and financial freedom works for everyone who employs it. Trying to get a lot of money right away with no effort is a plan that works for very few people. If you plan on acquiring a lot of money from inheritance, gambling, or crime, you are going to be disappointed.

Consider the numbers. Casino gamblers overall typically lose between $1 million and $200 million annually. The least-wealthy group of families receive, on average, about $6,100 in inheritance. People in the income bracket $25,000 to $250,000 a year inherit anywhere from $15,000 to $50,000. It is difficult for a person to spend the remainder of their life living on $50,000, which is not enough money to allow a person to quit their job and retire. Only the wealthiest 1% of families receive, on average, about $2.7 million in inheritance. As far as crime goes, you might get away with stealing money or robbing houses for a brief amount of time, but you will soon wind up in jail. The old saying "Crime doesn't pay" has been around for a long time for a reason. Any kind of crime is not an option for getting rich.

If you watch YouTube videos about wealth-building, success, and personal improvement, all these videos have ads at the beginning of them showing people who claim to have gotten rich overnight. These overnight millionaires want you to buy their Internet marketing plans or their secret formulas that promise you will be rich in months. The setting for these ads is a gorgeous tropical island or a multi-million-dollar house with an expensive sports car in the driveway. The reason they present their products this way is because so many people think being rich is all about having luxury cars, a huge house, and an expensive boat.

This type of product and marketing brings no value to anyone. These Internet multi-level or network-marketing schemes aren't selling a service or a product. The way these people are getting rich is by selling you their get-rich-quick scheme on the Internet. Their system is all about you selling the same false promise to another poor sucker. Most of these so-called lifestyle entrepreneurs who profess to have "made it" will be broke in two to five years because they don't have a product or service that brings any value to anyone. If these secret get-rich ideas were really that easy and fast, then everyone would be rich.

Only working smart and hard over time and bringing value to other people will change the amount of money a person regularly earns or has in the bank. To me, being wealthy means having the opportunity to bring value to other people through my products and services. I can take care of my family in any situation that life throws at me. I work where I want, when I want, doing what I love to do. My money works for me instead of me working for money, because I have harnessed my Six Life Assets.

PREMISE 3

The third premise of this book is if you want to live personally and financially free and stay that way, you must learn how to leverage your Six Life Assets. Every person on the planet has the same Six Life Assets. I believe the Six Life Assets are superpowers. That might sound crazy at first, but if you knew how much my life has turned around and continues

INTRODUCTION

to improve physically, emotionally, and financially because of my use of them, you would view them this way, too.

Your Six Life Assets Are:

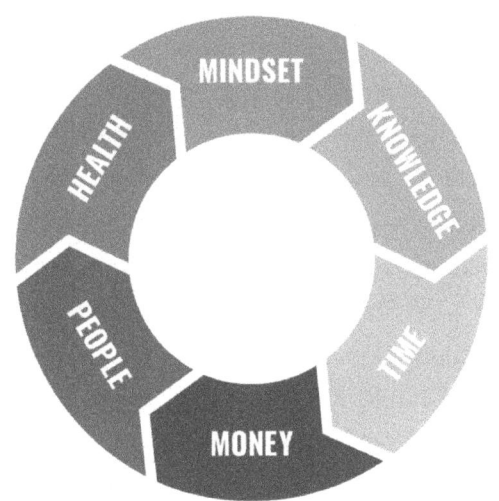

- **Mindset**
- **People**
- **Time**
- **Knowledge**
- **Money**
- **Health**

According to the website Investopedia: "An asset is a resource with economic value that an individual, corporation, or country owns or controls with the expectation that it will provide a future benefit. Assets are reported on a company's balance sheet and are bought or created to increase a firm's value or benefit the firm's operations. An asset can be thought of as something that, in the future, can generate cash flow, reduce expenses, or improve sales, regardless of whether it's manufacturing equipment or a patent." Examples of the Investopedia assets are physical property like real estate, cash in the bank, inventory, accounts receivable, stocks, and mutual funds.

Life Assets are not just physical things. Use this example to think about how Life Assets operate in my life every day. I purchased a 10-unit office building and a six-unit apartment building in just the past 60 days. My real-estate-brokerage team is poised to double in size this year. My marriage is the strongest it has ever been. My tennis game is better than at any other time in my life. I started working out with free weights again after 15 years of being absent from the gym. This is all happening for me because I guard and leverage my Six Life Assets.

For an asset to be one of the Six Life Assets, it must exist in every person's life, have a major impact on the quality of their life, and be necessary to become and stay personally and financially free. All of us, no matter where we live, how old we are, or whether we're already rich or still poor, have the power to benefit from our Six Life Assets. If we take the time to understand these Six Life Assets and learn how to use them properly, they can provide us with great economic value and future benefits.

The Six Life Assets work in concert with each other. Each asset can help develop, support, and increase the other assets. If any asset is not used carefully or wasted, it can reduce the value of the other assets. If you don't take care to have good health, then you won't have the energy to change your life. If you continue to waste time, then you can't grow your mindset or knowledge. If you stay broke and in debt, it will be hard to afford things like self-education or quality food to maintain energy and good health.

Most people have no idea they possess these Six Life Assets and have no idea about how powerful they are. If not used wisely, these assets can also have a negative effect on one's life. As I go through life and encounter people who are not doing well, I can see how their current quality of life is directly related to how they are not using their Six Life Assets. If they only knew how their life would completely turn around for the better they would just stop wasting these superpowers.

The goal of this book is to make people aware of what the Six Life Assets are, how valuable they are, how to gain control of them, and how to use them to become personally and financially free. The remainder of the book will cover each Life Asset in detail.

The chapter on Life Asset #1: Mindset covers this superpower, a foundational asset that jump-starts all the others. It explores techniques

INTRODUCTION

for changing your outlook on life, reducing your fears, expanding your comfort zone, and getting the Law of Attraction working for you. In Life Asset #2: People, we will explore how just one person can have an exponential impact on another person's life. We will analyze the different kinds of people in your life and how they help or impede your wealth-building and success. Life Asset #3: Time explains how to make your time work for you by replacing traditional time-wasting moments with positive habits of time management. The chapter on Life Asset #4: Knowledge provides the justification for and suggestions about making the space for self-education. Life Asset #5: Money gives critical strategies for getting control of your finances and making your money work for you. Finally, in Life Asset #6: Health, I use my own life experience to emphasize how our continual positive mental and physical health is essential as a springboard for our wealth-building goals.

I am a living example of what happens when a person works smart and hard over time, bringing value to other people. Now that I leverage my Six Life Assets, my health, happiness, knowledge, income, and net worth continue to grow every day. Harnessing the power of your Six Life Assets will be critical if you want to change your life and have personal and financial freedom.

◆ ◆ ◆

LIFE ASSET

#1

MINDSET

"It is not the critic who counts: not the man who points out how the strong man stumbles or where the doer of deeds could have done better. The credit belongs to the man who is actually in the arena, whose face is marred by dust and sweat and blood, who strives valiantly, who errs and comes up short again and again, because there is no effort without error or shortcoming, but who knows the great enthusiasms, the great devotions, who spends himself in a worthy cause; who, at the best, knows, in the end, the triumph of high achievement, and who, at the worst, if he fails, at least he fails while daring greatly, so that his place shall never be with those cold and timid souls who knew neither victory nor defeat."

—Theodore Roosevelt

"The things you think about determine the quality of your mind."

—Marcus Aurelius

There Is No Way to Do That

I *love the often-told story* of the two boys who were ice skating on a frozen pond. One of the boys fell through the ice and got trapped underneath. His friend started to frantically punch the ice but couldn't get through to save his friend. Out of desperation, he climbed a tree, broke off a large branch, and used it to smash the ice.

Eventually, the boy was able to break through and pull his friend out of the freezing water. Shortly thereafter, emergency services arrived at the scene. They were amazed and expressed wonder at how such a little boy was able to break off such a large branch, smash the inches-thick ice, and single-handedly pull his little friend out. As they shared their amazement, an old man walked up to them and answered their question. He told them: "The boy was able to do it because there was no one there who told him he couldn't."

We all have obstacles and reasons why we can't do something. I want to guide you on how to overcome obstacles, specifically those that prevent people from becoming wealthy. These barriers can be social, emotional, psychological, or financial in nature. By following the principles I outline, you will gain a solid understanding of the laws that govern wealth and learn how to shift your perspective on money and riches. Consider this your roadmap to transforming your mindset in order to achieve financial success. Our first stop is Life Asset #1: Mindset.

What Is Mindset?

If you want to change your life and grow wealth, the very first thing you must change is your mindset. Unless you truly believe in your heart and soul that you can be successful, that you can be wealthy, it will never happen. The change starts with your own thoughts.

Carol Dweck, a Stanford psychologist, defines "mindset" as a set of beliefs about our basic qualities, abilities, and potential for change. She explains that people with a *fixed mindset* believe that their intelligence, talents, and abilities are fixed traits. They believe that they are born with a certain amount of intelligence and that there is little they can do to change it. As a result, they may avoid challenges, give up easily, and be afraid of making mistakes.

On the other hand, Dweck says, people with a *growth mindset* believe that their intelligence, talents, and abilities can be developed through effort, hard work, and learning. They believe that they can always get smarter and better at things, even if they are not naturally gifted. As a result, they are more likely to embrace challenges, persist in the face of setbacks, and learn from their mistakes.

Put simply, mindset involves all the beliefs that shape your thoughts, words, and actions—how you move in the world. A *positive mindset* will allow you to wake up in the morning knowing you have goals to accomplish and work to do toward your better future. A *confident mindset* will help you take on bigger challenges knowing that you can learn whatever it takes to overcome them. This confident mindset will also allow you to interact with the people you must have around you in order to face these challenges—whether you're interacting as a leader, as a student, or as a peer. A *negative mindset* will come up with a hundred excuses about why something can't be done, and cause you to decide "it's not worth it" before you ever get started. The negative mindset pushes people away instead of drawing them in, or, even worse, it draws the wrong people close to you. A *scarcity mindset* will keep you from seeing the opportunity and the wealth available to you. If you decide from the very beginning that "there's just not any success/wealth out there for poor old me," it's not even worth taking a chance to grow yourself, grow your fortune, and become something new.

You will notice Life Asset #1: Mindset is the longest chapter. This is on purpose and for good reason. Your mindset is your "superpower asset." It will set the tone that affects all the other Life Assets explained in this book. If your mindset isn't right, it will be hard to get the other five Assets in line. I cannot stress enough how important this first Asset will be to you. To better understand mindset, let's look at some key ideas that form it: Law of Attraction, Your Why Statement, and the Essential Beliefs.

Law of Attraction

The superpower asset of Mindset is not a new concept. Numerous "principles for success" or "laws of the universe" have been around for thousands of years. CEOs, leaders, politicians, scholars, poets, kings, and conquerors all use these principles and laws of the universe to help them obtain their goals, run companies, build cities, conquer lands, and acquire great wealth. One of the oldest and most powerful of these laws is the Law of Attraction.

In 2006, a book called *The Secret* was published, which gained immense popularity. However, the concept it presented was not entirely new. The book was based on the Law of Attraction, an idea that scholars, historians, and leaders have known about for centuries. Even self-improvement experts like Jim Rohn, Earl Nightingale, and Zig Ziglar spoke about this law long before *The Secret* was written.

The Law of Attraction is the belief that, by focusing on positive or negative thoughts, a person brings positive or negative experiences into their life. The belief is based on the idea that people and their thoughts are both made from "pure energy" and that, through the process of "like energy attracting like energy," a person can improve their own health, wealth, and personal relationships.

The Law of Attraction is the single biggest reason my life has improved in many ways and my wealth and net worth continue to grow. My life turned around completely when I discovered the Law of Attraction and changed my belief systems. My life is proof you can start with nothing and become very successful when you learn to think like a rich person.

The Law of Attraction is not magic. It does not work instantly just because you become aware of it. It works overtime only if you live your life with the mindset of a positive, wealthy person—The Law of Attraction plus your Life Asset #1.

Your Why Statement

In addition to the Law of Attraction, another foundational support for your Life Asset #1: Mindset is a powerful **Why Statement**. Simon Sinek, in *Start with Why: How Great Leaders Inspire Everyone to Take Action*, says, "Very few people or companies can clearly articulate *Why* they do *What* they do. By *Why* I mean your purpose, cause, or belief—*Why* does your company exist? *Why* do you get out of bed every morning? And *Why* should anyone care?" This statement of purpose inspires not only us but also the people around us.

Passion and desire are very powerful emotions. They can motivate a person to get outside of their comfort zone and work hard to accomplish a goal or a mission. A *Why Statement* defines the reasons you want to work hard and change your life. Knowing why you want something and staying focused on that reason will have a huge impact on your chances of success. You need a well-defined positive *Why Statement* if you want to obtain financial freedom and build wealth.

My friend Mike decided to enter a body-transformation contest that was offered by the EAS supplement company. The winner of the contest would be the person who lost the most weight and had the lowest body-fat percentage after a six-month time period. Mike weighed 240 pounds at the time he started his transformation. He was probably 40 to 60 pounds overweight. Mike's typical weekend was sitting on a barstool at the bar my friends and I owned, drinking pints of Guinness. When Mike showed us the before-and-after photos of typical contestants and said he was going to win the contest, he was greeted with smiles and reservations about his chances. Over the next six months, he trained, ate, dieted, and ran like his life depended on it. He was obsessed with making a tremendous change and winning the contest.

Mike's transformation was miraculous. He lost 60 pounds, his body fat was in the single-digit range, and he was ripped like a competitive bodybuilder. Mike didn't win the contest, but he was a runner-up in his weight category nationally and won free supplements for a year. I will never forget his transformation. Mike's *Why Statement* was to turn his life around, become the healthiest person possible, and win the EAS supplement contest. His transformation is a testament to what is possible when a person has a very positive *Why Statement* and is passionate about fulfilling that *Why*.

A *Why Statement* does not exclude others. If you are passionate about what you will do for others as you grow your wealth and cash flow, it can drive you to unimaginable heights of success. A positive *Why Statement* that benefits others is important, because bringing value to other people is the foundation of acquiring great wealth. One of my all-time favorite self-improvement gurus, Earl Nightingale, said it best: "Your income is directly proportional to the value you bring to other people." Another favorite self-improvement guru of mine, Zig Ziglar, has a famous statement: "You can have anything you want in life if you help enough other people get what they want out of life." Other people matter, and, if you value them, you will experience that value come back to you.

One day I was asked by a real-estate client why I try to help people so much and why I am always trying to pay it forward. I do it because it is a key part of my personal *Why Statement*. Without even thinking, I said to my client: "The more people I help, the better my life gets!" Why do I do what I do? In my own daily meditation, I read my *Why Statement* in my mind to remind myself why I am trying to be the best person I can be and why I want to obtain financial success:

- "I want to acquire and maintain financial success so I can take care of my family in any situation life presents."

- "I want to acquire and maintain financial success so I can help other people change their lives, realize their goals, and enjoy financial freedom."

- "I want to acquire and maintain financial success so I no longer need a job and can work where I want, when I want, doing what I love."

Why do *you* want to have financial success and freedom? As you search for your own *Why Statement*, below are examples of other powerful and positive ones to inspire your own:

- "To keep my family safe, secure, and give them all the important things life has to offer."

- "To help rejuvenate and remove blight from an inner-city neighborhood."

- "To find a cure for cancer."

- "To invent a portable water-desalination system."

- "To improve aquaculture systems."

- "To start and own my dream company."

- "To start a company that responsibly competes in an industry or market segment."

- "To help a local charity purchase a building for their operations."
- "To pay for a vacation for my parents to visit their homeland."

The Essential Beliefs

Along with an understanding of the Law of Attraction and your *Why Statement*, these *Essential Beliefs* take your Life Asset #1: Mindset to its superpower status. If you want to change your life and grow your wealth, what you must change is your belief systems. Our belief systems are the foundation for where we are in life. Our health, happiness, accomplishments, and wealth are all controlled by our beliefs. Our belief systems shape our mindset, and our mindset controls our day-to-day actions and decisions. What we believe causes us to *think* and *act*, both of which are activities that create our reality.

When I think about my childhood, I remember moments when my father didn't support my dreams. Now, don't get me wrong: he was a hardworking person who always put the family first. However, he tended to be negative and would often doubt me or criticize my choices when I tried to step out of my comfort zone. No matter what I did, he would say I did it wrong. He didn't trust others and blamed everyone for his own life situation.

Given my relationship with my father, it might seem like I should have ended up a complete failure. And if you look at the first half of my life, it's true—I experienced many failures. I struggled in dating, dropped out of college, had unsuccessful business ventures, and even got fired from my first engineering job. I managed to wreck the first four cars I owned! I had a defensive personality and a negative outlook on everything.

So, how did I turn my life around from failure to success? Did I always have the right beliefs but didn't know how to use them? Or did I need to completely change my belief system? Well, it was a bit of both. Even as a kid, I always believed I could be successful and wealthy. This belief kept me going, even when life was tough and I faced repeated failures. I made plenty of mistakes, but I used them as learning experiences, always holding onto the belief that I could—and would—succeed. That one belief empowered me. As time went on, I gradually replaced negative beliefs with positive ones that contributed to my overall prosperity.

The *Essential Beliefs* fall into three categories: Believe in the Power of Belief; Believe in the Power of Yourself; and Believe in the Power of Change.

Category #1: Believe in the Power of Belief

Your "belief in belief" or really, your "belief in mindset," holds all the ideas in this book together. If you don't believe it, you won't see it. If you don't have faith that your new mindset will attract success, you won't take the steps. As Jim Rohn says, "The best of wisdom says this: Make plans like an adult, but believe in them like a child."

Whatever you believe is what will happen

> *"We become what we think about."*
> —Earl Nightingale

One important thing you should understand right now is that what you believe is what will likely happen. I can't explain why this is true, but it seems that the universe tends to bring into your life what you truly believe will happen. If you think positive things will occur, then positive things are more likely to come your way. On the other hand, if you expect negative things, then negative things tend to show up. This is a clear example of the concept mentioned earlier in this chapter—the Law of Attraction.

You can't fight against it, change it, or defeat it. If you choose to ignore this belief, your life will likely remain unchanged, and you won't have much control over what happens to you. Your current financial, happiness, and health status have been influenced by your beliefs. Understanding and being aware of this concept every day is crucial for the rest of your life. Without this belief, it's challenging to succeed in anything. It holds the key to transforming your life and achieving success in any endeavor.

This idea is so valuable that many self-improvement writers and speakers use this law to teach people how to transform their wealth, health, and personal relationships. If you want to get somewhere in life, you need to start acting like the person you want to become. You must accept the fact that your beliefs are controlling your life. And once you can accept that, what you can accomplish will be boundless.

Your potential is limitless

> "I want to challenge you today to get out of your comfort zone. You have so much incredible potential on the inside. God has put gifts and talents in you that you probably don't know anything about."
> —Joel Osteen

The movie *Facing the Giants*, about an underdog high-school football team, is a perfect example of the human will to succeed and how we are all capable of incredible accomplishments. In the famous "Death Crawl" scene, the head football coach blindfolds one of his players and asks him to crawl on his hands and feet across the playing field from the goal line to the 50-yard line, with another player riding on his back. Since a bandana covers his eyes, the player can't tell how close he is to the 50-yard line. Before long, the kid is complaining to the coach that he's exhausted. The coach gets down in the boy's face and yells encouragement, screaming, "Don't quit 'til you got nothin' left!" This tough-love tactic encourages the high-school boy to give his very best and to keep driving until he gets to his goal. The boy, sweating and panting and ready to give up, cries out that he has nothing left to give. But the coach barks, "Negotiate to find more strength!"

Finally, when the coach tells him he's made it and he can stop, the player collapses onto the ground, with the other boy still on his back. Panting hard and completely spent, the boy asks if he's made it to the fifty-yard line. The coach removes the blindfold and tells him the truth. He's crawled on his hands and feet across the entire 100 yards of the football field—twice the original distance the coach asked him to crawl and more than he ever would have thought possible.

You can accomplish anything you want in life. You possess the power to change and become anything you want to become. You can design and manifest any life you desire for yourself. It doesn't matter where you are in life right now or where you come from. Your current financial, mental, social, or geographic situation does not matter. You will discover as you go forward on your journey for success that your level of desire and the amount of effort you put in are the most critical factors. Your college degree, IQ, and resume have little or no bearing on whether you will be successful or not.

The "Death Crawl" scene in *Facing the Giants* reminds us of our limitless potential as human beings. Life has given us an incredible amount of talent. Unfortunately, most people never realize their true potential and hold themselves back by their own limiting beliefs. If you set your mind to something, give it your all, and never quit—and, most of all, believe in yourself—you will accomplish every goal and dream you have.

As the coach advises in the movie: "Don't quit... Don't walk around defeated... Don't waste your gifts." You have endless potential to fulfill every dream. Start growing your wealth right now by accepting the fact that your potential is limitless, and believe in *yourself.*

Category #2: Believe in the Power of Yourself

Once you solidify the essential idea that your beliefs about your world affect your world, look to yourself. Think about how the beliefs about your past, present, and future have affected and will affect your life. Ultimately, believing in yourself will provide a foundation for your future success.

It doesn't matter who you are or where you came from

> "The only person you are destined to become
> is the person you decide to be."
> —Ralph Waldo Emerson

To believe in yourself, start by looking at your beliefs about your past self. Every person has the potential to change their life for the better. It doesn't matter where you are financially, educationally, socially, emotionally, or even geographically. Success doesn't care where you come from or whether your family's name is impressive. Success does not care if you flunked out of high school or if you have a college degree. Success cares only that you are looking for it, that you want it worse than your next breath, and that you're willing to work for it. Success, wealth, and happiness are free and available to all of us. The belief systems, principles for success, and wealth-building knowledge to obtain anything you want in life are free—and they work for every person who will apply them.

If you weren't born with that silver spoon in your mouth, that's fine. It only means you must make enough changes that you can afford to buy your own silver spoon! For you, this might mean you need to get yourself out of debt or obtain more education. Maybe you want to land that perfect job or start your own business. Whatever your dream of success, it's there waiting for you to manifest it. Stop letting other people set your bar for you—rip that bar out of their hands, and set it as high as you want!

Characteristics like age, race, ethnicity, or gender have no bearing on a person's potential for success or wealth-building. Nor do things like sexual orientation, family status, or where your luck lies right now in terms of income, employment, or net worth. Yes, you probably have made mistakes in the past. But moving forward, you can still do whatever you want to do in this world if you have the will to try.

You must accept complete responsibility for where you are today

> *"If you could kick the person in the pants responsible for most of your trouble, you wouldn't sit for a month."*
> —Theodore Roosevelt

In other words, you are the only one responsible for your life. It's crucial to acknowledge that you have complete control over where you are today. Every aspect of your life, such as your living situation, credit score, health, income, debt, emotions, appearance, education, occupation, and relationships, is entirely within your hands.

If you're not satisfied with your current situation, it's not because of your parents, the government, or your employer. Most importantly, stop blaming life itself. Life hasn't been unfair to you, nor has it deprived you of luck. Life will give you what you give to it. It's as simple as that. Blaming others is an unproductive act that doesn't benefit anyone, especially not yourself. Only when you let go of the blame game can you create the mental space needed to start building the life of your dreams.

If you make poor choices and surround yourself with negative people, you will experience pain and hardship in life. However, if you make good choices, such as cultivating positive thinking, taking care of your mental and physical well-being, and seeking education, life will gift you with wonderful things. Stop complaining about not catching a break or waiting for your luck to change. You are where you are right now because of the choices you have made. Until you fully accept responsibility for your life, you won't be able to bring about any meaningful changes.

Nobody owes you anything

> *"A great burden was lifted from my shoulders the day I realized that no one owes me anything."*
> —Harry Browne

As you grow your belief in yourself, don't consider only your past self, but also think about the present. I don't care if your parents gave each of your siblings an inheritance and didn't give you anything. I don't care if all your neighbors won a million dollars in the lottery. I don't care if every one of your friends received full scholarships to Stanford and you didn't. Guess what? Life isn't fair. If you let it, life will keep kicking you until you decide to get out of the way of the kicking. If you are waiting around for something you think is owed to you, be prepared to keep getting kicked. Life will stuff you in a little box, close the lid, and put you on the shelf. The worst thing is that nobody will care.

No matter what has happened in your life, you need to accept the fact that nothing is owed to you. The world isn't at fault for where you are in life today and, by the same token, the world doesn't owe you anything. If you're waiting around for life to pay you back for something, it's going to be a long wait. The sooner you realize that your future is completely in your own hands, the better off you will be.

Stop holding out your hand for a freebie. It isn't coming. Your ship isn't coming in. The check isn't in the mail. The Marines aren't on the way. People who are more successful or wealthy than you don't owe you their sympathy or a free lunch.

It amazes me how people will try to convince someone who has more money than them to give *them* money or buy them things. When I meet someone who is more successful than me, my first thought is to buy them dinner or lunch, so that I can pick their brain. They are doing me the favor of sharing their knowledge, wisdom, and investment ideas with me. I'm the one who should pick up the check.

Another perspective that people have is that their employer owes them a pay raise just because they have been working the same job for the past ten years. This might come as a shock to you, but your employer does not owe you a raise. If you have been doing the same job for the past ten years without a pay raise, then you probably have not increased the value you are bringing to your employer. You are not worth more if you are doing the same thing you were doing ten years ago. Increase the value you bring to your employer, and then they will give you a promotion and a pay raise. They don't owe you more if you don't do more.

Instead of waiting around, just roll up your sleeves and get to work. You can take complete responsibility for your future. Start growing your wealth right now by accepting the fact that the world does not owe you a thing.

THE SIX STEPS TO LASTING WEALTH

You are in complete control of your future

> *"No one saves us but ourselves. No one can, and no one may. We ourselves must walk the path."*
> —**Buddha**

After accepting the Belief in Yourself regarding your past and present, use that same belief to help create your future. It doesn't matter where you are in life at this moment. You can be the type of person to sleep in or sit on the couch and watch Netflix all day—or you can get out of bed early and start changing your life. You have all the power and control, and nobody is going to make those choices and decisions for you.

You, and only you, are responsible for changing your own future. Only you can effectively make the necessary changes to improve your life. There is nothing and nobody in this world that is holding you back except you. You are the only person who can decide what happens tomorrow.

Once you've accepted that you and your choices are why you are where you are in life, then you are responsible for changing things to make your life better. You are the only person who can decide what happens tomorrow. Don't wait for your "break." You catch a cold or a ball—you don't catch a break.

The truth is every single person on this Earth has the chance to take their life to the next level. Lasting, positive change is possible for everyone who is willing to embrace the right mindset. The world-famous German-born diarist and World War II Holocaust victim Anne Frank wrote: "The final forming of a person's character lies in their own hands." Start becoming rich right now by accepting complete responsibility for what happens to you and the rest of your life—the future you will create.

MINDSET

Other people's actions and words have no effect on your decisions or your future

> "Your time is limited, so don't waste it living someone else's life. Don't be trapped by dogma, which is living with the results of another person's thinking. Don't let the noise of others' opinions drown out your own inner voice. And most important, have the courage to follow your heart and intuition."
> —Steve Jobs

I have been called delusional and grandiose because of the way I think. I see life much differently now. If there's nobody telling me, "It's too much, it's too difficult, it just can't be done," I consider it an honor because I've realized these comments are a stamp of success. Success is doing the things that most people won't even attempt.

The number-one sports team in each of the professional sports leagues is typically either loved or hated. Their fans love them, and the fans from all the other teams hate them—not because they are bad people, but because they are number one.

It may seem like talking about other people is really about *them*, but it is actually about what you believe about *yourself*. The day you stop worrying about what other people think or say about you and the choices you make is the day you can start increasing your happiness and abundance in all areas of your life. One of the most powerful shifts in thinking you can make is to start ignoring the naysayers and stop giving other people the power to make you feel bad.

The world is full of negative people who will make themselves feel good by making other people feel bad. You'll likely encounter these people as you make the necessary changes to grow your wealth. These people will say you are turning into a snob and trying to be someone you are not. They will say you're going to fail and lose everything. They will say you aren't smart enough. Whatever you do, don't lower yourself to their level. Don't criticize them back. They want you to fire back at them and become negative. In all circumstances, just let it roll off your back. These haters can hurt you only if you talk back to them or if they scare you into quitting. All this negative feedback from them is because they are scared and jealous.

Tell those who want to criticize that, if they'd like to be in your life, then they need to be supportive of your new goals. If these haters can't get on-board and cheer you on or even help you, then you might need to eliminate these negative people from your life. It will be hard at first, but it will be worth it.

The haters and doubters are going to show up. And, unfortunately, the people closest to us can sometimes be the biggest dream killers. They are jealous and feel bad because they don't know how to change their life. Our concern for what the people closest to us will say or think can cause more fear and paralysis than anything else.

The haters will slowly disappear, and you will start attracting positive people who will empower even greater change in your life. Remember, what other people say or do has no control over your future.

You must stop giving other people the power and permission to make you feel bad. Another person can say whatever they want about you—it is meaningless unless you give it meaning. We all have the power to determine how we feel about what other people say about us or how they react to what we are doing.

If you let other people's opinions, statements, facial expressions, or body language bother you, then you are giving away your power. If you are afraid of how other people will react to your goals or your dreams, you are just letting them steal your power. Don't be afraid of anyone. Keep your head down, stay in your lane, and take care of your business.

As the great stoic Greek philosopher Epictetus said, "If you want to improve, be content to be thought foolish and stupid."

Category #3: Believe in the Power of Change

It may seem contradictory, but once you have made the commitment to believe in the power of belief and yourself, you have to be willing to make changes. Sometimes we might view the need for change as a failure or a personal flaw. Actually, a willingness to change is showing your drive for growth and success.

Success requires change

> *"It's never too late to change your life for the better. You don't have to take huge steps to change your life. Making even the smallest changes to your daily routine can make a big difference to your life."*
> —Troy T. Bennett

Every a baby bird jumps out of the nest for the first time and flies. Even though they have never flown before and there is no guarantee that they'll be able to fly, they take that first tiptoe out of the nest and try it. They take the leap. If they don't, they won't become adult birds who can survive on their own—until they take that jump. Their lives won't start until they take that first scary risk of springing from the nest.

Once they make that leap—shall we say a leap of faith?—they never come back to the nest. It can be very scary springing out of your comfort zone to make a substantial change in life. If you aren't willing to change who you are, what you believe, and how you do things, then your life will not change. Your financial situation, health, and happiness reflect how you have lived your life so far. Even though change may seem daunting, you must be willing to change what you believe and how you do things. Only then will your life improve. Change is your friend.

Wealthy people embrace change and try to bring it about in their lives whenever possible because they know the secret: Only by pushing yourself to try new things and taking risks do you create change, experience growth, and enjoy prosperity. Once you get comfortable with it and learn that growing your wealth means changing many things about yourself, you will look forward to as much change as possible because it signals good things happening for you.

I'm speaking only for myself when I say I had to change almost everything I was doing before I could start down the path to financial freedom. I improved my thoughts, words, and decisions. I completely modified the type of people with whom I was surrounding myself. I changed the entertainment content I was watching and listening to. I even adjusted the foods I put in my body and when I went to bed.

So…you have a decision to make. If you want minor improvements to your life, then you will have to make some small changes. But if you want tremendous change in your life, then you must bring about huge changes in the way you think, act, and live.

I have learned to love change because I've witnessed the abundance that comes with it. These days, I'm not happy unless something in my life is changing. I feel trapped and bogged down when things stay the same because I realize change is what brings me growth.

What aren't you changing? Are you trying to repeat your parents' unsuccessful approach to wealth-building? Do you fear change? Change is inevitable and will require you to leave things behind. But when you learn to think and act like a rich person, change will be positive and exciting. Start growing your wealth right now by embracing and seeking change as often as possible.

Change will not happen overnight

> "The only place you find success before work is in the dictionary."
> —Vince Lombardi

I'm sure you've heard this adage: Do you know how to move a mountain? One pebble at a time! There is no secret process or shortcut to success. It comes with small, consistent changes every day that add up to massive changes over time.

You don't win, inherit, or steal success. Success is a lifestyle. Success is something you maintain. You don't buy success like you buy a car or a house. It is not a task, and there is no finish line. It takes working smart and hard over time to change any aspect of your life. There is no such thing as a secret formula for success, happiness, or wealth.

Once you've arrived at your own version of success, then it's up to you to maintain it. The famous bodybuilder, actor, and politician Arnold Schwarzenegger said he built his life and success on "sets and reps." And the highly successful college basketball coach John Calipari famously expressed, "You have to learn to love the grind!"

Bill Gates and Warren Buffett, two of the richest people on the planet today, live the lifestyles of people who are continually building wealth. They will most likely continue to do this until the day they die. Why? It's what they do. They understand the philosophy of building wealth over time, accepting it, believing it, and buying into it. Wealth-building requires patience. There is no shortcut to success and happiness. It takes time and effort to change your life. And it's not a one-time job—it's a way of life.

Many people incorrectly believe that rich people are born with the Midas touch or that they somehow got "lucky." All the rich people I know have earned their fortune by working smart and hard over time bringing value to other people. If you want to be able to think like a rich person, then you must remember that luck—or the lack of it—is not your problem. Instead, your belief systems have power—they have the power to lift you up and out of any situation.

Billionaire Warren Buffett started his wealth-building lifestyle at the age of 9, when he first began studying the stock market. He lived with the mindset of wealth for his entire life and finally made his first billion when he was 64 years old. Ray Kroc, the founder of McDonald's, didn't open his first McDonald's store until he was 56 years old. Similarly, Bill Gates quit college when he was in his early twenties to start Microsoft in his garage, and then didn't take a vacation for 20 years as he worked on developing his company. These billionaires did not get lucky; success was not handed to them. Instead, they earned every penny by working tirelessly over time, surrounding themselves with the right people, believing they could do it, and never quitting.

Another close friend of mine, who built his success on his car-dealership business spent 20 long years working on his company. Again, he didn't just wake up one day to find someone had put a pot of gold at his door. Another friend and client took 15 years to build up his 900-unit rental-property portfolio. Even though he was able to quit his full-time job at the age of 35, he still works every day with a wealth-building mindset.

Creating wealth is a journey and a lifestyle, and it takes time, patience, and perseverance to fully engage in this way of life. Please don't fall for the false promises of get-rich-quick programs, of which there are many. I have never met anyone who has used those plans and succeeded. The only person getting rich from those ideas are the people selling the idea. Trying to find that pot of gold at the end of the rainbow is a popular get-rich philosophy these days. These deceptive programs involve doing little or no work and putting in minimal time and/or requiring none of your own money. If these business concepts worked, then why isn't everyone rich today?

I know many investors who work hard every day to acquire massive wealth over time. I have never met someone who drastically changed their standard of living with some secret formula—or without considerable time and effort. This is the most important message I can convey to you. You are not going to get rich overnight. It just doesn't happen. It takes time and effort to change your life. If you are serious about changing your financial place in life, then you should embrace this philosophy.

Start growing your wealth right now by accepting the fact that working smart and hard over time, bringing value to other people, is the only way to acquire and maintain real success and wealth.

Don't let a setback stop you from changing and moving forward

> *"It's the breakdown before the breakthrough."*
> —Michael Maher

A setback is an event that occurs in all our lives. Setbacks aren't something we cause intentionally or maybe even cause at all. Setbacks, whatever their source, are unpredictable. They happen every day. They range from things like getting a flat tire, to dropping your cell phone into the toilet, to breaking a body part or being the target of a frivolous lawsuit.

Sometimes, setbacks are serious and make us doubt ourselves and our life course. Success suicide is a type of setback that happens to people when they try to change their life and pursue big goals. It can be in the form of a physical injury, sudden accident, or even a self-destructive decision that happens to you right before all your hard work is about to pay off.

Success suicide comes in many forms, but it generally happens when you are starting to see progress from all your efforts. It can be health problems, an accident, or a natural disaster. Success suicide is life's way of testing how serious you are about becoming successful. So many people let it derail their goals. The thing to never lose sight of is that success suicide is temporary. If you stay the course, don't quit, and work through it, life will reward you with your goals and dreams.

Now is the best time to start changing your life

> *"Procrastination is one of the most common and deadliest of diseases, and its toll on success and happiness is heavy."*
> —**Wayne Gretzky**

If you want to be rich, then stop wasting time. *Carpe diem*—seize the day! If you want to change your life, then there is no better time than the present moment to do it.

So many people suffer from "analysis paralysis." They make every excuse in the book to keep from taking chances or having to put in the extra work necessary to pursue their dreams. The clock never stops ticking, so you better get going right now. Stop waiting and making excuses. Procrastination is keeping you from living the life you deserve.

There will never be a better time to start changing your life. Next week or next year will not be better or easier. Between now and then, life will present other hurdles. Don't wait until the kids are done with college or your divorce is final. Don't wait until you get some bill paid off or your tax refund arrives. All the opportunity, abundance, money, and technology are waiting for you—right now. Now is the best time to start changing your life. Start growing your wealth now, and stop putting off pursuing the life you deserve.

MINDSET

You either grow or you die

> *"Step out of the history that is holding you back. Step into the new story you are willing to create."*
> —Oprah Winfrey

On the surface, this belief might sound a bit cruel. How can it be that your life is either getting better or getting worse, but not able to remain in its current state?

Most people seem to be happy with the way their life is, and they don't believe they need to change it. They love their job, their family, their dog, and the weekends playing golf and swimming in their pool. Their current annual income allows them to pay all the bills, contribute to their 401(k), and take an annual vacation.

This sounds perfect. If it isn't broke, don't fix it. Right? Unfortunately, today we live in a rapidly changing world. The rising cost of living, negative climate change, and the still-unknown future impact of emerging technologies are going to create massive change across the globe. The growth of Artificial Intelligence, robotics, automation, the global economy, and the pending implementation of blockchain technology alone will drastically change the employment landscape over the next few decades. Economists predict the elimination of millions of jobs due to all this change.

The increased cost of food, transportation, education, housing, and healthcare has far outpaced the increase in workers' compensation. If your income stays the same, then you are becoming poorer just due to the rising cost of living. Financial analysts predict that 40 percent to 60 percent of people will not be able to afford to retire. If your job can be replaced by a robot or kiosk, your income hasn't significantly changed in several years, or you have been performing your job with the same skill set for the past 5 years, then it is time for you to realize you are dying, not staying the same.

> Looking for more explanation or examples about how working with change can drive your success? Find out more in my Change Is Good resource here:
> *https://www.selfmadewealth.co/resources*

The Power of Your Mindset

I'm sharing these belief systems with you now because I truly believe they'll help you find success. If you apply the principles, then money will follow you. It will gravitate toward you because you will think, act, and talk like a rich person. All the money you need to be successful has already been printed and is available to you. The fact that it's not in your possession right now . . . well, that's only a minor factor. It won't determine whether you obtain success and wealth.

I will always use myself as a notable example of what can be accomplished with the right mindset and working smart and hard over time to bring value to other people. My parents had no money and worked minimum-wage jobs their entire life. My father did not finish high school, and my mother had only a high-school education. I grew up across the street from a bar and two blocks from the railroad tracks. I was a bad student all through grade school, high school, and college. I flunked out of college after one year and made every relationship, money, education, and job mistake a person could make. Then, my life turned around completely when I changed my belief systems. My health, happiness, and wealth have been growing ever since. My life is proof you can start with nothing and become very successful when you learn to think like a rich person.

It's not just me. You may have people in your life who have undergone this transformation. Several of my close friends started out in humble circumstances but are now multi-millionaires. These guys started with no money in their pockets but "somehow" became wealthy. A good friend of mine went to prison for selling drugs. When he was released, he went on to receive two college degrees, start several businesses, become a social entrepreneur, and earn much well-deserved regard in his community. Another friend I grew up with in my neighborhood got his high-school degree and then completed a four-year enlistment in the Army. His family wasn't wealthy and didn't hand him a huge inheritance, yet he was able to begin a thriving business by working smart and hard over time. He began washing cars for a living and then got his car-dealership license. Fast forward twenty years, and he is now a multi-millionaire who owns several lucrative dealerships, a profitable stock portfolio, and numerous income-producing real-estate properties.

The one thing they all have in common is that they achieved all of this by believing they would succeed, not caring where they were from, working smart and hard over time, and bringing value to other people. You can change your life and become rich if you are willing to take the first step and do the right things.

Building a Powerful and Resilient Mindset

Now that you understand more about what mindset means and what it includes, I want to show you some simple strategies to start you on your path. You will also find links to short courses and workbooks that are completely free to the person reading this book—the person who wants to take the steps to live in success.

Visualization

Visualization is a powerful technique in which you create detailed mental images in your mind. By imagining yourself achieving your goals or facing challenges, you can boost your confidence and motivation. Athletes use it to practice and improve their performance mentally. It's a useful tool for students, too, helping them excel in academics and reduce stress. Just visualize success, and it can have a positive impact on your mindset and achievements.

I've heard many success- and wealth-building gurus say that, if you want a big house, you should drive through the neighborhoods where those homes are as often as possible. If you want an expensive car, then drive around those car lots and see your dream car. I call this the *"See-it, touch-it habit."* If you look at the object of your desire often enough, you will eventually start taking steps to acquire it.

Looking at magazine pictures of places you want to visit, watching videos of things you want to accomplish, and following successful people online who have started the business you want to start is a fantastic way to get motivated. For years, I would look at fly-fishing magazines to see the awesome photos of trophy fish being caught in exotic, faraway locations. Now I take those trips every year. I went to Alaska for a week of fishing in August 2015. It was an epic trip. I went to Kiritimati Island in the South Pacific in February of 2018 for some of the world's best bone fishing. Whenever you get a free hour, go to a bookstore, and spend some time looking at magazine photos of the things you want from life, like surfing, fishing trips, real estate, travel destinations, etc.

My wife and I frequently vacation in Rehoboth Beach, Delaware. On the drive from Erie to Rehoboth, we pass through Lancaster, Pennsylvania. I have always wanted to own a modern cash-flow-producing self-storage facility. One of the greatest indoor climate-controlled facilities is in Lancaster. Every time we take the trip to Rehoboth, we get off at the

Lancaster exit, where Supreme Self-storage is located. I go to the property and get out and walk around the building. I love seeing this investment property. I'll even go inside, walk around the interior, and take photos if the door is open. It is the self-storage facility of my dreams, and I know someday I will own one like it. Examples of the visualization habit include:

- Drive by the investment property you want to own.
- Tour Open Houses of the homes you want to live in.
- Visit the business you want to be in.
- Look at magazines with photos of the goals you want to reach.
- Watch YouTube videos or TV shows that show you the objects of your desire.

The *"See-it, touch-it habit"* has paid huge dividends for me. It is one of the best visualization techniques to get you motivated toward living the life of your dreams.

Fishing on Kiritimati Island and Alaska

Vision Boards

A vision board is another type of visualization technique. It is a graphical representation of your dreams, goals, ideas, passions, and *Why Statements*. It is a collection of photos, drawings, text, and images that you can use to remind yourself of what you are working for. Looking at images of your goals and dreams will stimulate and strengthen your thoughts. It creates more positive energy, which helps trigger the Law of Attraction in your life.

Hang your vision board on a wall that you walk past frequently—this could be in your kitchen, bedroom, or office. This is a great way to view your visual goals and dreams every day.

Start by writing your *Why Statement* at the very top of your vision board. It might read something like this: "*I want to get out of debt and obtain financial freedom so that I can start a community college that teaches underprivileged residents how to work in the building trades.*"

Then write down some words or phrases that describe your goals and dreams. These could be phrases like: Financial Freedom; Vacation Home; Debt-Free; Community College; or even Mercedes-Benz. Make sure these words are bold and in large text, so that you can read them from a distance.

Next, add photos of your loved ones or the people whose lives you want to change when you make your dreams a reality. Last of all, add photos of what you want to obtain from life. By looking at your vision board on a regular basis, you will keep the things you want to have, do, or be at the front of your consciousness. It will not be long before your wishes start coming true.

Hang your vision board someplace you will see it several times a day. Make a point to look at it when you first get up in the morning and before you go to bed at night.

> Looking for more explanation or examples? Find out more about vision boards here: *https://www.selfmadewealth.co/resources*

Meditation

More and more successful, wealthy entrepreneurs are realizing the value of regular meditation. Meditation helps reduce stress and keep you focused on what is important. It helps you not to worry about the past or too far out into the future. Meditation before you go to bed will calm you down, reduce anxiety, and help you fall asleep at night. It is good for your physical and mental health. Meditation about positive events, gratitude, and affirmations creates positive energy, triggering the Law of Attraction. I highly recommend ten to fifteen minutes of meditation every day.

A technique I use to involve my subconscious mind and leverage visualization is a six-step meditation thought process right before I go to sleep at night. After I am lying in bed with all the lights out and preparing to fall asleep, I close my eyes and perform the following five thought processes:

First, I use controlled breathing to help me reduce any stress or anxiety that has accumulated during the day. Controlled breathing is a great way to decompress after a long day of work and play. I take ten deep, slow controlled breaths. I recite in my mind as I breathe in the words "Calm in." I recite in my mind as I breathe out the words "Worry out." Controlled breathing helps settle me down and prepare me for sleep.

Second, I use the concept of gratitude to review all the wonderful things in my life I am thankful for. Even the comfortable bed I am lying in. The food I ate that day. The love I gave and received from family and friends. I express my gratitude for the day for all the simple things we all sometimes take for granted.

Third, I do what I call my confession. I apologize for anything I did that day that was inconsiderate, possibly made another person feel bad, or generated any negative energy in my mind and body. This confession allows me to generate more positive energy and remove any negative energy from the day. We are all human, and we make mistakes. We all do things that might not be nice. If I cut someone off in traffic or looked at another person and made a judgmental thought in my mind, it is not nice, and it generates negative energy. I ask for forgiveness for anything that was mean or not nice. I always feel better after I spend a minute reviewing what I could have done better that day.

Fourth, I read my *Why Statement* in my mind to remind myself why I am trying to be the best person I can be and why I want to obtain financial success:

- "I want to acquire and maintain financial success so I can take care of my family in any situation life presents."

- "I want to acquire and maintain financial success so I can help other people change their lives, realize their goals, and enjoy financial freedom."

- "I want to acquire and maintain financial success so that I no longer need a job and can work where I want, when I want, doing what I love."

Fifth, I recite my goals with intention, which will support my *Why Statement.*

- "I will own fifty income-producing rental properties."
- "My real-estate brokerage will have a team of thirty successful real-estate agents."
- "I will own a profitable education business based on book sales, seminars, and paid speaking engagements."

Last, and most importantly, I imagine in my mind how I am already living the life of my dreams. One of my goals is to spend an entire summer in Rehoboth Beach, Delaware, writing my next book. Rehoboth Beach is a small town right on the ocean in Delaware. Rehoboth Avenue leads down to the boardwalk on the ocean, and I enjoy spending time in the cafes and eateries.

In my mind, I imagine sitting in the outdoor seating at The Mill coffee shop or one of the great Crepe shops. The sun is shining, and the air is warm. I'm wearing a T-shirt, shorts, and flip-flops. I already hit the gym that morning and had a great breakfast. I can smell the salt air from the ocean, and someone walks by and smells like suntan lotion. My coffee tastes awesome.

Set Goals

At the same time you are using different visualization techniques to support the *Essential Beliefs,* you also want to be setting and working toward your goals. Goals are clear ideas of what you want to accomplish. They represent where you want to go. Even if you don't know how you are going to get there, it is critical that you clearly define where you want to go.

Goals are central to achieving success in any endeavor: business, sports, education, relationships, etc. I truly believe that writing down our goals is something we should all do. I almost always obtain the goals I write down, whereas I usually don't obtain the goals I don't write down.

After years of my own personal research, I've narrowed down effective goal setting into ten steps:

1. Make your goal realistic.
2. Make sure your goal is specific and well-defined.
3. Set a specific time period or date to accomplish the goal.
4. Put your goals in writing.
5. Break your larger goal into a set of smaller goals.
6. Read your goals out loud to yourself every day.
7. Decide what you will sacrifice to accomplish your goal.
8. Determine when you will work on your goal.
9. Create a system to track your progress.
10. Find someone to hold you accountable.

Goal setting is a substantial part of my life, and it has allowed me to achieve much success. Along with effectively setting goals, you need to cover a variety of areas: health, education, relationships, sales, marketing, experiencing life, hobbies, personal finance, investment, and income. I've used these specific goal categories to accomplish remarkable things. These categories constitute areas of my life in which I always want to grow because they lead to empowerment and wealth. This type of thinking and goal setting will help you grow your wealth.

Goal setting is truly a key component to actualizing your mindset and fulfilling your personal intentions for success. This list will get you started, but take advantage of the free, valuable resources I provide to expand your potential to reach your goals.

> **Looking for more explanation or examples?**
> **Find out more about setting goals here:**
> *https://www.selfmadewealth.co/resources*

Journal

Journaling is like having a nightly conversation with my inner self. It's not just about recording the day's events or jotting down ideas; it's an intimate dialogue where I dissect my thoughts, decisions, and feelings. The thing is, people often get intimidated by journaling, thinking it has to be this literary masterpiece. But the truth is, it doesn't need to be complicated. It's about getting what's in your head onto paper, not creating a bestseller. Simplicity is key. It's in the reflection, the raw honesty with yourself, that you find those golden nuggets of insight and growth. Journaling is incredibly liberating. It's as if every entry peels away another layer, revealing a clearer, more-focused version of myself.

The methods available for journaling are more versatile than ever. Whether you're a tech-savvy individual or someone who enjoys the classic pen-to-paper method, there's a platform that's just right for you. Take Google Drive, for instance. It's not just for spreadsheets; you can pour your thoughts into a doc and have access to it anywhere you go. If you crave the tactile connection, nothing replaces the feel of a high-quality paper journal. And let's not forget the middle ground—we've got apps designed specifically for journaling, brimming with features that can help you delve deeper into your self-discovery journey. You've got options like Evernote and OneNote that give you the digital-notebook experience, blending the best of both worlds. And don't sleep on audio notes; sometimes just voicing your thoughts without any filter can give you a fresh perspective. So don't get stuck thinking journaling is one-size-fits-all. Tailor it to fit you; make it your own unique ritual.

The way I journal is through a tool I invented called The Money Playbook. This tool combines the previous suggestions of visualization, vision boarding, and setting goals into a journaling method. This method, a real ace in the hole in your arsenal of life-changing techniques, has helped me manifest and acquire all forms of happiness, money, health, personal achievement, and investment assets. If you want to build a house, you need tools and a blueprint. If you want to start a company, you need a business plan, systems, and processes. If you want to find buried treasure, you need the treasure map. In the same way, if you want to change your life and become rich, you will need tools, systems, plans, and maps.

The Money Playbook is all those things and more. It has been the blueprint for change for me and can be for you. It's too big to explain in full in this book. But don't worry—you can access the full explanation, with examples, free for you.

Putting It Together

Life Asset #1: Mindset is the foundation, the super asset, that drives the remaining 5 Life Assets explained in this book. The other assets will inevitably support your mindset development—an educational experience will give you new strategies to try, or a person you meet randomly will become a transformational mentor. *But*, until those things start happening, *you* have the control to sculpt your mindset to be one that will help you reach your goals for life success and wealth generation. Even if you notice some of those things happening for you before any adjustment, Life Asset #1: Mindset will be the solid and continually developing piece that will sustain and support you.

Strategies to Develop Life Asset #1: Mindset

While this chapter has set the foundation for the rest of the assets, there are some key takeaways and activities to get you started *today*:

- Five quick things to do right now:
  - Drink more water
  - Get at least seven hours of quality sleep every night
  - Read at least thirty minutes a day
  - Stop watching negative TV and the Internet
  - Avoid negative people
- Reflect on the Essential Beliefs. Where is it hard for you to buy in? What examples in your life or others' lives prove them to work?
- Begin to develop the habits of visualization, vision boarding, and meditation. These will help you develop the all-important super asset of Mindset.
- Set written goals! Use the free resources to expand your knowledge of goals and execute the writing of your goals.

- *Extra Credit*: Work through the Money Playbook at the QR code below.

> **Looking for more explanation or examples?**
> **Find out more about setting goals here:**
> *https://www.selfmadewealth.co/resources*

◆ ◆ ◆

LIFE ASSET
#2

PEOPLE

SURROUND YOURSELF WITH THE RIGHT PEOPLE

"Surround yourself with those who only lift you higher."
—Oprah Winfrey

When I was a freshman in college, I became friends with a bunch of guys who were on the university's golf team. They were great guys, and we had a blast together. Unfortunately, we had a little too much fun. We spent more time drinking and having fun than going to class and studying. I had a 0.6 grade point average after my freshman year. I was kicked out of school midway through my sophomore year.

After I was asked to leave college, I got a job with a construction company, digging ditches and pushing wheelbarrows of concrete around. Talk about back-breaking work! Fortunately for me, many of the kids I grew up with in my neighborhood were more studious than me, and they were succeeding at college. They didn't get kicked out of school for partying. As my friends were growing up with their college experience, making new friends, and talking about their futures, I was not growing. My friends were surrounding themselves with other successful college students. I was working with a bunch of older guys who were suffering from bad backs due to lengthy careers in the construction industry. I was growing apart from my friends down the street from me, whom I had known almost my entire life, and I did not like this pattern. We just were not on the same page anymore, socially or intellectually. I was jealous of this growth they were experiencing, and I did not want to lose my friends. The thought of losing close lifetime friends is what motivated me to cut out the partying and go back to college.

I applied and was accepted to the Rochester Institute of Technology. I graduated from RIT with a bachelor's degree in electrical engineering. It was a challenging program for me because I was never a good student. I always struggled to get good grades. When I went back to college, I was serious about getting my education and graduating.

To help me get good grades and make my life easier, I decided to observe what the smart kids were doing and try to emulate them. I perceived several traits of most of the smart students. They always sat up front, they never missed class, and they typically studied with other smart people. According to Tony Robbins, "If you want to be successful, find someone who has achieved the results you want, and copy what they do—you'll achieve the same results."

This quote worked perfectly for me when I was at RIT. I started sitting in the front row in every one of my classes. I never missed class, no matter what. Third and most importantly, I joined a study group with other students who were serious about meeting weekly to study and share solutions to all the homework problems. The results were incredible. I made the Dean's list that semester.

Once you adjust your mindset, articulate your *Why Statement*, and buy into the *Essential Beliefs*, you are ready to develop your next Life Asset—the people you surround yourself with. Your choice of people to live with, fall in love with, play with, work with, and invest with will be some of the most important decisions you will ever make. The people in your life you spend time with have more impact on your chances of changing, growing, succeeding, being happy, and building wealth than any other factor.

Who Are "My People"?

Sports are a metaphor for life. Think about the most successful professional athletes. They are surrounded by the best coaches. They have stadiums full of raving fans, with professional cheerleaders cheering them on from the sidelines. They play in stadiums with comfortable locker rooms, state-of-the-art fitness centers, and professional rehab staff. You need to start living your life as though you are a professional athlete and ask yourself the following questions:

- Who is your coach?
- Where are your fans?
- Do you have cheerleaders?
- What is your stadium environment like?

It is critical to consider who you are letting into your life, because just one person can completely change it. This works both ways. Just one great mentor can send you down a path toward health and wealth that you could not have imagined! In the same way, one wrong, toxic person can completely derail you. If you are truly serious about changing your life and growing wealth, then you must assess the people in your sphere of influence.

I spent the first half of my life surrounded by people who came to me by default. My first friends were the people who lived in my neighborhood.

The other people who came to me by default were the members of my immediate family. None of us can change who our parents, siblings, or other relatives are. We have no choice about the family we've been born into. Your "sphere of influence" is a term used to describe all the people you spend the most time with. Most of us probably develop our sphere of influence simply through association by default. Most people enter our lives because we are related to them, we work with them, live next door to them, or sit next to them at school.

If you think about it, for the first fifteen to twenty years of our lives, we meet people by default. It is completely random. The first people we all meet are our parents, when we are born. Next, we meet our siblings and relatives. When we are old enough to go outside and play, we typically play with the kids next door or down the street. That is our only option if we want to make friends. On top of that, our parents tell us right before we go outside, "Don't talk to strangers." That is good advice when we are children but not so good for later in life. What happens when we start school? Typically, we get close to the kids in our classroom, especially whoever sits next to us. When we get our first job, we get to know all our fellow employees and the people sitting or working nearby or eating lunch at the same time in the breakroom.

In the first fifteen to twenty years of our lives, we are just not taught to think about who we surround ourselves with. It is completely random and chosen for us. We haven't deliberately chosen to be around these people. This happens to all of us, and it's okay. But if you want to change your life and grow your wealth, going forward, you must consider who you spend your time with and how they affect you. Once you start doing this, you'll really be able to step forward toward thinking and acting like a rich person.

We have six basic types of people in our lives:

- Mentor/Coach

- Team Member

- Cheerleader

- Neutral Person

- Critic

- Toxic Character

Who Are Mentors and Coaches?

Finding a mentor or a coach should be your number-one priority when you are changing who you surround yourself with. A mentor can be a person who has an exponential impact on your personal growth. They can truly help you change your life.

A mentor is a person who has a high level of expertise in their field or industry. This is someone who demonstrates ethical behavior and concern for others. This sort of person both gives back and pays it forward. Mentors have a teaching mentality and share what they know with others. They have a proven track record of success, as well as a positive attitude. Mentors help others believe in themselves.

Warren Buffett makes a good point about success: "It is okay to learn from mistakes; just make sure they are someone else's." Finding a good mentor is an effective way to learn from other's mistakes and successes. I have spent most of my life without mentors, learning everything through trial and error. As they say, I attended "The School of Hard Knocks." One of the main reasons I am writing this book is to share everything I have learned the hard way, so that you don't have to go through the headaches and heartaches I have endured in my life.

I teamed up with my lifelong best friend in my first business partnership. After twelve years of doing business together, we realized we were never on the same page when it came to managing employees or money. When money got tight, we started fighting, and our relationship came to an end. Unfortunately, I didn't know anything at the time about creating legal-partnership documents, which would have included a buy-sell agreement and a dissolution clause. This would have helped me immensely when we decided to go our separate ways. As it was, we had no structure in place and went through a nasty business breakup. Miserable, I spent a lot of money and lost a lot of sleep for three straight years.

If I had had a mentor when I'd gone into business with my friend, my mentor would have guided me through the business decisions I needed to make, both at the beginning of my business and as I navigated through the murky legal waters. I was flying blind and had no idea what I was doing. I ended up losing money, time, and my best friend. This was an expensive and painful lesson for me.

A good mentor would have encouraged me to surround myself with a business team of professionals, like an attorney, insurance agent, real-estate agent, accountant, banker/loan officer, and financial planner. Having trusted professionals like this would have ensured that my ventures were successful and that I was protected as an individual. These key professionals would have mentored me in their areas of expertise and kept me from the problems I faced. They also can prevent people from losing money, getting sued, or having problems with the IRS.

A good mentor can do many positive things for you. One good mentor can change the course of your life. Some of the ways a mentor can have a positive impact on your life:

- Save you from trial-and-error and learning things the hard way

- Fast-track your expertise in a certain area of life or business

- Provide motivation and hold you accountable

- Loan money to you to start your business or purchase an investment

- Help you find private lenders

- Help you with strategic decisions, planning, and goal setting
- Help you find investment deals
- Introduce you to other mentors
- Suggest educational resources, seminars, books, etc.

So how do you find this trusted mentor? Ask a successful friend, relative, co-worker, boss, or neighbor. People you already know are usually willing to help you. Another idea is to join a club. If you're interested in real-estate investing, you could join your local landlord association. Or you could take part in an investment club. How about joining a service organization like Rotary International or Kiwanis? You could join your local Chamber of Commerce, which often holds networking events that could help you find the trusted mentor of your dreams. Business Networking International and Toastmasters are both great organizations for surrounding yourself with successful people. Clubs are not only a fun place to meet people who have the same ideas, motivations, or goals you have but also an excellent place to find a mentor.

If you want to surround yourself with like-minded people who are trying to build wealth and become rich, then joining an organization is something to consider. Chances are, most of the members have had a mentor at one time in their life. Usually, they are willing to return the favor by helping someone like you. When it comes to success and growing wealth, you don't need to reinvent the wheel. You can avoid a lot of mistakes by learning from these people. Find where the wealthy people and investors are meeting, and gain access to that group of people.

If you like to golf, then become a caddy at the country club in your region. Successful high-net-worth people like to golf. If you don't golf, then get a job cleaning the locker rooms or waiting tables—just get yourself in the door of the club. Get a job at the local yacht club performing a service for sailboat owners. People who own sailboats are typically well off. Find a job at the tennis club. People who can afford to play tennis at a club are typically successful investors, high-paid professionals, and business owners. Do whatever it takes to get your foot in the door. Clean the floors if that is what it takes to get access to these potential mentors.

Read your local newspaper, and see who is making headlines. Figure out who is making waves in the way you'd like to make waves. If you're interested in becoming a real-estate investor like me, find out who's purchasing property in the region. Who's involved in development projects?

If you are intimidated by reaching out to someone you don't know, then try the approach I use every day. This approach is one of the best ways to find a mentor to help you grow wealth. It is free and available to anyone who wants to use it. It is open 24 hours a day and never denies you access. It is called the Internet. Today, there is more information flowing freely across the Internet than ever before. Entire libraries of data and educational materials are waiting for you. Podcasts, YouTube videos, and online blogs and articles are bursting with information on how to change your life and build wealth. Stop watching shows like *Lost*, *Breaking Bad*, *The Originals*, and *Game of Thrones*, and get serious about educating yourself so you can grow wealth. Below is a list of people who produce my favorite podcasts or YouTube videos or have written life-changing books. At this time in my life, I consider these people to be my mentors:

- Patrick Bet-David (Valuetainment)
- Tom Bilyeu (Impact Theory)
- Eric Thomas
- Earl Nightingale
- Jim Rohn

PEOPLE

- Les Brown
- Tony Robbins
- Zig Ziglar
- Pat Flynn (Smart Passive Income)
- Tim Ferriss
- Codie Sanchez

When you're looking for a potential mentor, ask yourself a couple of questions. First, is the person ethical? Make sure you select a mentor who is honest and can be trusted. If they are not fair and honest with other people, then they won't be honest with you. You need to have a very high level of trust with your mentor.

Does the mentor you have in mind have a positive, happy attitude? You want to spend time with a mentor who is happy and positive, because one of the benefits of having a mentor is that they will motivate you to succeed. If a person has a negative attitude and they are always complaining and criticizing other people, then, chances are, they won't be a good mentor.

It's also quite important to make sure the potential mentor has experience and success in the field or industry you want to pursue. If you want to become a bodybuilder, then join a gym where all the best competitive bodybuilders go. If you show up every day and ask them for advice, you'll learn their strategy. If you are trying to build wealth, you can't take advice from a person standing in the unemployment line. You need to find people who are successful at building wealth if you want to become successful at building wealth. In the same way, the most important thing is to find a mentor who has already succeeded at whatever it is you want to achieve in life.

When it comes to selecting a mentor, you want to play up in life! When you ski behind a good skier, you start to ski better. When you play tennis with better tennis players, you start playing better tennis. When you hang out with investors, entrepreneurs, and happy, successful people, your life will change for the better—you will think, act, and make decisions like these successful mentors.

How do you approach a mentor? The simplest way to recruit a mentor is simply to ask them if they will mentor you. One of the most basic needs of people is to feel important. When we ask another person for help, they feel important. If you ask another person to mentor you, chances are, they will feel complimented by your request and might agree to help you. You should still be ready to offer something in return for their help. The right mentor will have a great attitude and enjoy helping other people. They might agree to mentor you just because they'd enjoy the challenge of helping someone less fortunate.

However, be ready for all types of responses. It might go something like this: "Why should I mentor you? What are you going to do for me?" If Warren Buffett or Bill Gates called me tomorrow and asked me to work for them for an entire year for free and in exchange, they would mentor me, I would drop what I am doing and go running! That would be an opportunity of a lifetime. You need to be prepared to offer something in return for your mentor's guidance and expertise.

If you find a great mentor and they want you to do something in return for mentoring services, I suggest you offer anything you can that is legal and ethical to become their student. Offer to be their personal assistant, marketing person, landscaper, or housecleaner. Offer to do research for their company or latest business idea. Offer to wash and wax their car for a year. I'm not kidding! How badly do you want a great mentor? If you find a truly great mentor, they can alter your future in so many great ways that cleaning their car or house for free for a year will be a drop in the bucket compared to what they are going to do for you. Remember, they don't need you—you need them!

Another way to find a mentor is to hire one. Before you dismiss this idea of paying another person to help you grow your wealth, consider that we pay for other kinds of lessons. We pay for tennis, music, driving, or swimming lessons. Why is it that, when it comes to one of the most important aspects of our future—money—we don't invest in any education? I will never understand that. Rich people hire the best and most-expensive accountants, tax consultants, and investment advisors because they know they are investing in their net worth and financial freedom.

Every year Warren Buffett auctions off a one-hour lunch with himself for charity. In 2017, an anonymous bidder paid $2.68 million dollars for that lunch date. I doubt if lunch with any human being is worth that much money, but I think you get the point. Rich people will pay other rich people for advice and coaching.

Who Are Team Members?

Another person who comes into your life is a team member. These folks want to see you succeed and are willing to act and invest their time and money in your mission and dreams. Team members can provide valuable resources that can be the difference between success and failure.

A team member might be a spouse, sibling, parent, relative, friend, co-worker, or employer. They can provide a place to live, advice, motivation, financial support, or money. They might not be a mentor, but they could possibly know and introduce you to someone else who could be a mentor.

One of my best friends, Ray, moved to York, Pennsylvania, to live with his uncle while he started a car-detailing business. Ray's uncle put a roof over his head while he got his new business venture off the ground. Twenty years later, Ray is a multi-millionaire with several car dealerships and a cash-flowing rental-property portfolio. I would say that his uncle was one of Ray's early team members who helped him on his road to success.

In my own life, I've enjoyed having team members. For instance, I was able to purchase several profitable rental properties with money friends and colleagues (a.k.a. team members) lent me. I would not have been able to make those acquisitions without the help of these people who believed in me and wanted to help me.

Don't forget the people who help you, and try to return the favor someday. If they lend you money, always pay it back, no matter what the situation. Under no circumstances should you burn a bridge with a team member.

Who Are Cheerleaders?

Cheerleaders help bolster you, especially when you are doing the hard work of changing your mindset and growing your wealth. This is a person who may not have the resources to be a team member, but they want you to succeed just the same. A cheerleader can be a spouse, sibling, parent, relative, friend, co-worker, or employer. Your mentor and team members will also be some of your best cheerleaders! The other people I mentioned will be more readily available than your mentor, and you need both sources of cheerleading.

Emotional support is very helpful when you're trying to make changes in your life. Some people will always doubt you, so that's why it's important to counter that with positive energy and support from your cheerleaders, who want you to succeed. Cheerleaders will be happy for you if you reach your goals. There will always be times when you need someone to tell you that you are doing the right thing and not to quit when the going gets rough.

Who Are Neutral People?

Neutral people are just that: neutral. They aren't mentors, team members, or cheerleaders. They are not detractors, either. Neutral people are typically siblings, parents, or spouses. They don't say much when you tell them you plan on changing your life to become successful and to grow wealth. These folks don't weigh in one way or the other. Telling them about your plans really doesn't matter to them. They are neither negative nor positive about your goals. Don't try to force a neutral person to be a mentor, team member, or cheerleader. Neutral people are usually neutral because they don't want to be involved due to their own fears, or they don't want to take any risks. When it comes to neutral people, let sleeping dogs lie.

Who Are Critics?

Unfortunately, the world is full of critics. These are the people who will doubt you, and, more than likely, you know many of them. The closest people to you are usually some of your biggest critics. They will be your spouse, siblings, parents, relatives, friends, co-workers, or employers. Critics don't stand in your way, but they will take every opportunity they can to tell you how you are making a mistake or wasting your time and that you aren't capable. They might even share your goals and plans in a negative way with other people or on social media. Be prepared for their criticism and negative talk.

Some classic statements from critics are:

- You aren't smart enough!

- You weren't born rich, and you never will be!

- You are going to lose your money!

- Oh, now you think you're too good for us!
- You are selling out!
- Those new friends of yours are just using you!

Critics will put you down for two reasons. They are afraid for you, and this is their way of trying to stop you from what they think is a bad idea. The second reason is that they are jealous you are doing something they don't have the confidence to try themselves.

Either way, you have several choices when it comes to handling critics. You can tell them to stop with the criticism, get behind you, and become a cheerleader. The second choice is to ask them to say nothing at all and be a neutral person. The third choice is to remove the critic from your life and not spend any more time around them. This can be a difficult choice to make if the critic is someone close to you. But, if their criticism is holding you down, it might be time to let them go so that you can fly to your dreams.

Do not allow a critic to linger in your life because you are afraid to confront this person. One critic can have a constant negative effect on you and become a dream killer.

Who Are Toxic Characters?

Toxic characters lead toxic lives and surround themselves with other toxic people. These people get into trouble, live unethical lives, and even break the law. They typically abuse substances like drugs and alcohol. Toxic characters tend to be confrontational and even violent. They make themselves feel good by making other people feel bad. They will go out of their way to hold you back or set you up for failure. They might even be abusing you emotionally, physically, or socially. You can't trust these people, and you must completely and permanently remove them from your life.

It is unlikely you will be able to change a toxic character. If you associate with someone like this, you must get serious about inviting them to move out of your life. If it is your spouse, sibling, or parent, you will have an extremely difficult decision to make. It is almost impossible to change your life if you are spending any time around toxic characters. They will set you up for failure every chance they get. This will never change. You cannot become successful and grow your wealth with these people surrounding you.

Examine the Current People in Your Life

We all have influencers in our lives who tend to fit into one of the categories just explained. We need to be aware of the role these different people play in our lives. Motivational speaker Jim Rohn famously said that we are the average of the five people we spend the most time with. In the same way, our happiness, health, and wealth will be the average of the people we spend most of our time with, as well.

Who Are My Influencers?

If you are reading this, you most likely do not live in a vacuum. We all have people we share lives with: those we spend multiple hours a day with. Because of this, these people will influence us. These will be the most influential people in your life: your partner/spouse; your boss/co-workers; your parents, siblings, and relatives; and your friends.

Partner/Spouse

Who you choose as your life partner is understandably one of the most important decisions of your life. You will spend countless hours with them, know them intimately, and share some of your most vulnerable moments with them. Nobody is perfect, but choose and commit wisely.

When it comes to deciding who your life partner is, you don't have to look any further than that person's relationship with their siblings and the quality of their parents' marriage. If their relationship with their siblings is adversarial, confrontational, or contentious, then their relationship with you is going to be the same. If they act a certain way with their own flesh and blood, then it's likely they aren't going to treat you any better. Make sure the person you choose to commit to is a person who loves and trusts their siblings and wants to be around their family.

Our family history and the environment we grow up in have an impact on how we live, play, and work with other people. We are the products of our environment. Our compatibility level, communication skills, conflict-resolution skills, and positive or negative attitude are hereditary. Though these personal attributes can be worked on and improved, you are taking a big chance if you think you are going to change someone.

Since this person is someone you'll be spending most of your time with, you need to think about their attributes and tendencies. If your romantic partner can't manage their money, then, eventually, you'll be sharing their debts, and they will be wasting your money, too. Similarly, should your life partner neglect their health, you may find yourself in the role of their personal caregiver or facing the financial burden of their healthcare expenses. Or worse, you'll take on their exercise and diet habits and feel physically poor yourself. Your life partner can have a profound impact on your future.

Boss/Co-worker
Is your boss or your employer helping you grow? Make sure your boss is your biggest cheerleader. He or she should be a mentor and always willing to help you do better. It's best to work for people who want you to succeed.

This might sound obvious, but many supervisors out there want you to be only good enough to get your work done. They don't want their staff members to do *too* well, because it might make them look bad. They also don't want you to grow as an employee because you might be considered for a promotion before them. Many supervisors are where they are because of the Peter Principle: They have risen to the level of their incompetence. These bosses will always set you up for failure.

The same concept applies to your co-workers. Try to find people you work with who are engaged in their jobs and the work they do. So many people today act like they hate their jobs, and it shows. They sit around bashing the company and their boss every chance they get. Stay away from these people. They are bad for you and give off a ton of negative energy. Stay clear of the complainers.

There are great benefits to socializing with co-workers who have a positive attitude, want to make a difference, and care about the quality of their work. First off, you will learn more about the company's business processes, possible job openings, new job skills, etc. Second, you will have a positive image in the eyes of the people who own or run the company. Third, if there is a downturn in business and the company needs to lay people off, I can assure you that the employees who do all the complaining are always the first to go.

Aim to work for a company and a boss that wants you to grow and succeed. Find a company with growth opportunities that provide training and educational benefits. Once you're there, hang around with those co-workers who are most positive and happy to help you live your best life. You might have to change jobs if you determine that your boss, company, or co-workers are having a harmful effect on your life or your attitude.

Parents, Siblings, and Relatives
The people who have known us the longest—our family—are the toughest groups of people to analyze and change. We are born into this circle of people, and we cannot change that fact, no matter what we do. Another reason this is such a critical group of people is that, regardless of how

much time we spend with them, their thoughts, comments, and opinions have a big effect on us.

Unfortunately, the people related to us can be the most negative about our goals and dreams. They are often the ones who warn us against taking any chances. They might tell us we'll lose all our money or that we're not smart enough to accomplish anything. If they aren't 100% behind you, don't discuss your dreams with them. Make sure that, when you're sharing your plans with loved ones, they're supportive. If they won't help you or at least be your cheerleader, then keep them out of the loop. They need to be happy for you—not jealous or negative.

If you trust these people, then ask them to be cheerleaders, team members, or mentors to you. If you already fear what they will say, and you don't trust them, then keep your goals and dreams to yourself. Minimize the time you spend with them and the information you share with them. If you feel you must tell them about your goals and plans, then only share information after it has been accomplished or completed. If you plan to attend a seminar on starting an online business, share this information only after you attend the seminar or start your new business. This way, they can't talk you out of it with negative comments.

Friends
Friends are another tough group of people to analyze and change because we have typically known our friends for a long time. If you trust your friends, then ask them to be cheerleaders, team members, or mentors. Just as with your family, if you fear what they will say, and you don't trust them, then keep your goals and dreams to yourself. Reduce the time you spend with them. If you feel the need to share your goals and plans, consider sharing only *after* you've achieved them. If you don't trust your friends to support you like cheerleaders or teammates, it might be a good idea to find new friends who will be more supportive. You can always make new friends.

If you want to change your life, you're going to need to analyze and possibly change many aspects of what you're currently doing. Finding friends who have a positive influence on you is a good place to start. This might sound like a hardened view, but if you feel you need to change your life in a significant way, then you should consider if the friends you're spending time with are good for you.

How to Analyze Your Influencers

With Life Asset #1: Mindset, we talked about the power of change in becoming successful and growing wealth, and now we need to apply it. This next section will provide some tough questions to use for reflection. You might not *like* the answers, but you should consider them in order to support and grow in the important Life Asset #2: People.

Let's start with this analogy: The winner of a bass-fishing tournament is the boat that catches six fish with the heaviest combined weight. For example, if your boat catches six fish weighing one pound each, then your combined weight at the end of the tournament is six pounds. If you were to catch six fish weighing two pounds each, then your combined weight is twelve pounds.

At the start of the fishing contest, the anglers try to catch any six fish they can as soon as possible. After they have six fish, their goal then switches to increasing the total weight of their six fish. When they catch a seventh fish, if it weighs more than any of the six fish they currently have, they release the lightest fish they're currently holding in the live well of their boat and keep the new one they just caught. This increases the total weight of their six fish. As the day goes on, they continue to replace light fish with heavier fish.

You might be asking yourself what this has to do with the people in your life. Before this next part, I want to remind you that this may be uncomfortable. What I'm suggesting is, just like in the fishing tournament, you might have to "throw back" some people if they are hurting you and not making positive contributions to your goal of changing your life. The goal is to replace the people who are hurting you or holding you back with new people who want to help you. People are a huge Life Asset in your life, and they can help you do incredible things. Unfortunately, they also have the power to hurt you tremendously.

Always try to motivate the people in your life to be cheerleaders, team members, or even mentors if they have mentor qualifications. If someone is a critic, then get them to be neutral, or get them out of your life. Most toxic characters will not change, so be prepared to get them out of your life at all costs.

When it comes to letting people into your life, you need to adopt the mindset of an employer. If you owned your own company or small business, you would not hire the first person who walks through your door. You wouldn't hire your neighbor just because he or she lives next door to you. You might not even hire your best friend unless they meet your qualifications. Employers spend billions of dollars every year on human-resource departments, human-resource professionals, software, and candidate-screening processes. They want the most talented staff so that their company can succeed, grow, and be profitable.

You need to take the same time and care when you decide who you want to let into your life. Your life is like a business, and your friends, family, co-workers, employer, and mentor are like your employees. They can make or break you. This approach to deciding who you spend time with might sound cold and calculated. That's because it is very calculated, and you need to remove your feelings and emotions, and just use logic. It's up to you if you want to change or stay the same. You can't change your life unless you change the people in it.

It is important for you to take some time to think about who your influencers are and how they work in your life. Here's an exercise for you. Make a list of the people you spend the most time with. It can be family members, relatives, friends, or co-workers. It doesn't necessarily have to be five people, as Jim Rohn suggested. It can be three people, or it can be ten people. The key here is to determine who you are spending the most time with. This is the list of people who are going to help you or hurt you on the path to your dreams. You must know who they are and then analyze their effect on you.

Write down the names of the people you think are influencers, and, next to their names, write down the role (mentors, team members, cheerleaders, neutral influences, critics, or toxic characters) each of these people plays in your life. In another column, write down what role you wished they would play for you.

Your list might look something like this:

NAME	CURRENT ROLE	FUTURE ROLE
James	Cheerleader	Team Member
Janet	Critic	Neutral Person
Raymond	Neutral Person	Cheerleader
Beth	Team Member	Mentor
Jim	Team Member	Team Member
Sarah	Neutral Person	Cheerleader
Sally	Critic	Neutral Person
Bill	Toxic Character	Avoid or Remove

Make sure everyone in the list above is a person you spend a lot of time around or a person whose comments or opinions have a big effect on you. The reason they are on the list is that they have a strong impact on you, in one way or another. Because these are the people who have the biggest influence on your life, they also impact your chances of changing and becoming rich.

In analyzing these people, consider whether there's anything you can do to improve the role they play for you in your life. If the person is good for you, then maintain the relationship as it is. If the person is harmful for you, can you encourage them to be more helpful to you in some way? If not, consider minimizing the time you spend with them or even removing them permanently from your life. Tim Ferriss, an American entrepreneur, author, and podcaster, said this: "A person's success in life can usually be measured by the number of uncomfortable conversations he or she is willing to have." You might have to conduct some uncomfortable conversations to improve or remove the influence of the people in your life.

Below is a list of questions to ask about the people who have the power to influence you in your life and what kind of effect they are having on your chances for change and success.

Financial questions to ask yourself about each person on your list:

- What is their annual salary?
- Do they own any assets, like real estate, stocks, or a business?
- What is their net worth?
- What are their financial liabilities?
- How much money have they saved over the past year?
- What is their plan for retirement?
- What is their debt level and credit score?
- Have they ever been foreclosed on or claimed bankruptcy?

PEOPLE

Growth questions to ask yourself about each person on your list:

- What is their education level?
- What is the title of the latest book they read?
- How do they spend their free time?
- Do they have any goals?
- What is their current employment status?
- How long have they been at the same job without a promotion?

Personal questions to ask yourself about each person on your list:

- Have they ever been arrested?
- What are they like when they have been drinking?
- Do they drink too much or too often?
- Have they ever cheated on their spouse?
- How do they treat their children, spouse, siblings, parents, and friends?
- How do they talk about their children, spouse, siblings, parents, and friends?
- What is their health like?
- Would you be afraid to share your goals and dreams with this person?
- What will this person tell you when the going gets rough or when you start to fail?

- Do they complain a lot?

- When they find out about your goal of becoming rich, what will they say?

- If you asked them for help, would they offer it?

- As you make the changes in your life and move toward becoming rich, how will they feel if you succeed?

This is an uncomfortable set of questions to ask. You might love the people on your list and truly enjoy the time you spend with them, but the people you surround yourself with will have to change if you want to reach your goals and grow your wealth. This is not negotiable. The people you spend time with have a direct impact on your net worth and income. If you are not currently rich, then you are hanging out with the wrong people.

The Chain of Events

Surrounding yourself with successful people has a multiplying effect. One good thing leads to another. When good things happen, usually even more good things happen. You gain momentum when you are around the right people. This philosophy is part of the theory that the rich get richer and that it takes money to make money. If you hang around successful people, then success will follow. There is an inevitable chain of events that occurs from your association with each person in your life. It is either a positive chain of events or a negative chain of events.

Babel, a movie starring Brad Pitt, is about how one decision a person makes sets in motion a chain of events that can affect another person on the other side of the world. There is a scene where a young boy in Morocco, Yusef, accidentally shoots his sister, Ahmed. This decision sets in motion a chain of events that ultimately leads to the death of a tourist in the United States. Yusef's father, Ahmed, is arrested for the crime, and the tourist's wife, Susan, is left to care for their young son, Mike. The two families are brought together by tragedy, and they learn to understand each other's cultures and perspectives. The scene shows how the decisions that we make, no matter how small, can have a ripple effect that reaches far beyond our own lives. It is a reminder that we are all connected and that we need to be mindful of the impact that our actions have on others.

This premise is so true when it comes to surrounding yourself with the right people. Being around another successful person can expose you to a concept, a piece of knowledge, a new method to perform, a task, an important lead, or a great investment opportunity that can have an exponential impact on improving the quality of your life.

In the summer of 2006, I found myself taking a cruise on a 50-foot yacht at our local yacht club. The owner of the yacht is a very successful and well-known business owner and entrepreneur. The other passengers on the yacht were all very accomplished as well. I felt very fortunate to be in the company of such a successful group of people. I just sat there while the owner of the boat and a local multi-millionaire real-estate developer talked about some major developments taking place in the local region. I was giddy inside; I was getting access to this kind of information just because I happened to be on the boat that night! As I sat there on that million-dollar vessel, taking in a perfect evening (and eating prime rib!), I asked myself how I got there. I could not afford to join the yacht club, let alone own a 50-foot yacht. I wound up in that very desirable situation because of the conscious decision to surround myself with successful people. It was a chain of events that was the result of getting to know one successful person.

The very first real-estate office I worked in had a senior real-estate agent named Bill. Before I became a real-estate sales agent, my business partners and I had a building we wanted to sell. I called Bill because I'd seen his name on so many "For Sale" signs on buildings in the area. Since it looked like this man was a successful realtor, I called him for his opinion about our building.

I gave him a complete set of information about our building and asked him to get back to me with a suggested price. A week later, Bill called me and said the information I gave him was very impressive and I should consider becoming a real-estate agent myself. This suggestion set in motion a chain of events that has culminated in my owning my own real-estate brokerage and becoming the president of my local Rotary Club, accomplishments I'm very proud of. This entire chain of events happened all because I met Bill.

When Bill asked me to come into his office to see what they did, I accepted his invitation. When I arrived, I saw some impressive cars in the parking lot: an Audi, a Mercedes-Benz, a BMW, and a Lexus! Everyone inside was well-dressed, and photos of all the commercial property the brokerage owned decorated the walls. It didn't take long for me to realize that this was a place where I could surround myself with successful people. I knew that, if I worked hard, some crumbs would fall off the table, and I could pick them up.

To say I picked up a lot of crumbs during the time I spent working at Bill's office is an understatement. It is amazing how just one successful person can set off such a dramatic, positive chain of events in your life.

Unfortunately, the same can be said for a long-term association with one wrong, negative person. Surrounding yourself with successful people really pays off.

Putting It Together

Once you commit to personally developing your mindset in a positive way, your remaining Life Assets have the power to add (if done well) to that development. Putting yourself in situations to meet the people who will support your goals and fostering those relationships will help you reach new levels of success and grow your wealth in ways you never thought possible. I am not telling you to get rid of everyone in your life, but you need to add people. Going through the difficult process of really considering who are the "right" people to surround yourself with goes a long way toward creating the life you want.

Strategies to Develop Life Asset #2: People

You understand how to lay your foundation of Mindset from the previous chapter. Now, you can add to that knowledge; here are five takeaways and activities to get you started *today*:

- Find a mentor

Reach out to someone after your life analysis, or find a professional mentor online.

- Attend seminars and conferences

People who attend seminars and conferences are excited about changing their lives, so these are the people you want to be around. Their positive and forward thinking is contagious, and it will rub off on you, motivating you to climb to new heights. These events have speakers who are already successful at what you want to accomplish. They give talks and sell products to help you reach your goals. You will make connections with these people, forging relationships that will have a positive impact on your goals and life.

- Join a business or investment club

Find the local landlord association or investment club if you want to become a stock or real-estate investor. These clubs are eager to welcome new investors and provide educational programs, networking events, and important resources.

- Join a service organization

Find your local Rotary or Kiwanis club. These are humanitarian clubs that give back to the community. Their members are typically business owners and investors, who are great people to surround yourself with since they typically have successful, positive attitudes. These clubs are a good place to find a mentor.

- Join a networking group

Networking groups can be in person or virtual. BNI (Business Networking International) is a networking group you pay to join, but you get to be around business owners and professionals who are trying to grow their businesses and income. If you ask around, you might find other, less-formal networking clubs with professionals in your area. Use Facebook or Google to find something that meets your needs.

◆ ◆ ◆

LIFE ASSET
#3

TIME

*"You cannot save time, find time, or make time.
You can only stop wasting time."*
—Joe Herbert

"The trouble is you think you have time."
—Buddha

Though it depends on genre, typing speed, and number of writing sessions, there is no doubt that it takes quite a long time to write a book. In fact, the average time is about 180 days. When I decided to write this book, I did it while I was working 60–70 hours a week starting my real-estate brokerage. I knew that if I didn't carve out time to dedicate to the process, I wouldn't finish. I decided to go to bed at 9:30 p.m. every night and get out of bed at 6 a.m. every morning. From 6 to 7 a.m. every morning, I worked on making this book a reality. After work, I would do laundry, buy groceries, go to the gym, etc. I felt that the time from

9:30 p.m. or later was wasted time. It was too late to work on the book, and the gym was closed. I don't like shopping for groceries at midnight. I just shifted my day and used any time after 9:30 p.m. to sleep so I could start my day earlier. This shift alone had an enormous impact on my ability to complete the book that you are reading today.

How many times have you heard the following statements: "I need to make time for that," "I just can't find the time," or "If you do it this way, you can save some time"? So far, we have set up the "superpower" asset of mindset. We've also learned the necessity of cultivating the relationships around us so we can maximize our support system. But, what drives our days, weeks, months, and years is time.

Every person possesses different amounts or levels of the six Life Assets, except time. Time is the only Life Asset we all get the same amount of, and that never changes. The richest person in the world and the poorest person in the world are both given twenty-four hours a day. One of the big differences between successful people and unsuccessful people is what they do with their time. Rich people use their time to make money, self-educate, improve their lives, have fun, and help other people. How we decide to use our Life Asset #3: Time is one of the major factors that will determine if you can change your life and become rich.

Unfortunately, most people do not value their time because it is free. We get twenty-four hours for free at the start of every day, whether we ask for it or not. *In Time*, starring Justin Timberlake, is a film demonstrating what would happen if time was not free and each person had a limited supply. The movie is set in a future where people stop aging at 25. The downside is that they live only one more year after that. If a person wants to live longer, they must barter and pay for more time. In this alternative world, time is the ultimate currency. As we think about growing wealth with the 24 hours we are given, it would be wise to treat time more like a currency.

If you are not rich, and you want to become rich, then you must be willing to change almost everything about your life, especially what you do with your time. Here's the hard-but-essential truth: Whatever you spend a lot of time doing, that is what you will be good at. If you spend a lot of time lifting weights, then you will develop strong muscles. If you are like Warren Buffet, you spent decades studying bond charts and stock-market data to become a stock investor worth billions of dollars. Successful people spend a lot of time perfecting their skills and companies; that is why they become good at it. They did not get lucky. Their success was not handed to them. They put in the hours over the years.

If you practice the habits of poor people over and over, then you will most likely remain poor. Just wanting and wishing to be rich will not change anything. You need to start using your time doing the things rich people do. This chapter will help you look at the ways we use time and how we can better utilize it to grow wealth.

Where Does All the Time Go?

If you can figure out how to make, find, or save time, you will become the richest person in the world overnight. If you're like most people, your life is already busy with work, school, family, kids, and taking time out to have fun. You are probably asking yourself how you will be able to fit anything else into your busy schedule so that you can start changing your life. The goal and challenge are to change what you already do with your time.

Our time fits into a few general categories, with some more controllable than others. Each of us needs to figure out how much time we're spending in each category and consider which activities contribute to our success, happiness, and health—and which of them do not.

The following list is a breakdown of the main categories of how people could use their time.

Daily Necessities (Very important, but you have less control)

- Sleeping
- Eating
- Working for money
- Hygiene and health
- Unexpected interruptions, emergencies, and accidents

Daily Options (Important, and you have more control)

- Unavoidable time wasters
- Life maintenance
- Entertainment
- Socializing
- Self-education
- Creating passive income and building wealth

After considering all these areas, I have reached the point where I want to choose from only four daily options with my time: self-educate, make money, have fun with friends and family, and help people less fortunate than me.

The Bare Necessities

In the categories for organizing time, our daily necessities include: sleeping, eating, working for money, hygiene and health, and unexpected interruptions. We know these things are necessary to function in the world. We know that there are inevitable challenges and problems we might face every day. But even with these certitudes, we can use the time within them more efficiently and effectively.

Sleeping

Sleep is not negotiable when you are trying to free up time to change your life. You can't ask someone to share their sleep with you or loan you some sleep or sleep on your behalf. There is nothing to leverage with sleep. You must perform this action on your own with your own time. I don't recommend sleeping less so you can free up time. Sleep is important for good health, motivation, and focus.

We all struggle with sleep sometimes. If you can't sleep, don't fight it. Get up and read, watch YouTube, or work on your business. Sometimes when I can't sleep, it's because I'm anxious about work, money, or investments. When I get up and journal about what is bothering me or take notes on how I will rectify the problem, my mind feels easier, and I can go back to sleep.

Making the most of the necessity of sleep is also about adjusting your schedule to make your awake time productive. "The early bird catches the worm" has been around for a long time because it's true. Make the following time-schedule adjustments to your life: Go to bed early, around 10 p.m. or earlier, and start getting up early. The bottom line is that you will be successful if you have a longer day rather than a longer night.

There are numerous reasons to go to bed early and get up early:

- You will be mentally recharged, in your most creative state of mind.
- The outside world does not get up early, so you will have minimal interruptions.

- Once your workday gets going, it is too hard to stop and self-educate or build and create your product or service.

- You will start freeing up time to change your life and become rich.

- You will be acting like a rich person.

- Studies show that the later you go to bed, the unhealthier you will be.

Don't want to get up early? Neither did I. I live in a cold, northern climate. Getting out of bed at 6 a.m. wasn't the easiest for me until I discovered a few tricks to make it easier. I bought myself a warm robe and slippers and set a timer with an oil-filled electric space heater that heated my room 30 minutes before it was time to get up. I also used a timer to turn on a soft nightlight 15–30 minutes before I was due to wake up—this helped my system get used to the idea that it was almost time to get out of bed. Once I was out of bed, I would drink a pint of water, spend 10 minutes writing down some affirmations, and practice gratitude to jump-start my day with positive and creative thoughts.

If you want to change your life and pursue becoming rich, you are either going to do it on the front end of your day or the back end of your day. You are more productive, less tired, and less distracted at the beginning of the day.

Eating

We have to nourish our bodies as a daily necessity, but there are ways to do it that help us value the time we spend doing it. It's true that time can be saved in this category if you eat nothing but fast food. I recommend that you continue to eat (because not eating will make you sick as well), but take the time to eat good, healthy food. The CDC explains that adults who follow a healthful diet not only have lower risks of certain cancers, diabetes, heart diseases, and obesity, but they also live longer and are better able to manage chronic conditions. I have days when I am jammed up with tons of appointments, or I'm running late, so I run through a drive-through for a sandwich, but this happens only once or twice per month. I try to eat food that improves my health and allows me to perform at peak levels. Food matters when you are trying to build wealth. Healthful food is fuel for success.

Acquiring and preparing food is an interesting subject today, with all the online business startups focusing on food preparation and delivery. One way to maximize your time is to let someone else do the planning, prep, and sometimes cooking for you. These businesses offer versatile, reliable, and healthful choices. If you consider how fast, predictable, and reliable the logistics of shipping have become, having your food delivered to your home is a great option for freeing up time.

Working for money

Whether you work for an employer or you are self-employed, you'll most likely be spending at least 40 hours per week generating earned income. This might be tied to a specific location or to certain hours of the day. What takes place during this time might not be directly in your control. There's not much most of us can do to free up time here, at least until we build our passive income enough to no longer be dependent on a job.

Hygiene and health

Hygiene and health are somewhat like sleep, in that you can't ask someone to do this for you. Hygiene and health are not mandatory like sleep, but I highly recommend you don't cut these activities out of your life to free up time for building wealth. You can stop taking showers, shaving, brushing your teeth, and working out, but I doubt it will draw success to you. Personal hygiene affects your self-confidence and prevents the spread of many illnesses. You can ignore the chest pains you have been experiencing and skip the doctor's appointment, but you will probably keel over and be taken to the hospital. Be productive in using your time wisely in this area, and you may actually add time to your life overall.

Unexpected interruptions, emergencies, and accidents

Unexpected interruptions, emergencies, and accidents are a fact of life. Sometimes we can minimize the amount of time these events take and the impact they have on our lives, but these things are going to happen to us all. Poor people *and* rich people will experience these events. Call it fate or karma, but life's unexpected events do not favor or discriminate toward any of us.

What successful people have are *contingency plans* in place to minimize the impact these inevitable events have on their lives. The goal of these plans is to reduce the financial and time loss incurred when these events do happen. Join AAA, an Internet-based navigation and security service, and be sure your car insurance covers what you need for driving-related emergencies. Make sure your life-insurance policies and those of your close loved ones will be adequate when this unfortunate event hits close to home. Be sure your phone regularly goes to the lock screen and has a backup of important credit-card, bank, and password information in the event of personal, home, or cyber theft.

Also, consider your own weaknesses you may have labeled as "unexpected interruptions." Maybe you tend to speed. Save yourself some time (and money)—you won't get any speeding tickets if you don't speed. I tend to lock myself out of the house, sometimes up to five times a year. To help overcome this potential timewaster, I have a Realtor's lockbox somewhere on the exterior of my house with a spare key in it. Can you imagine if I had to call my wife to come from work to let me the house every time I forgot my key? What a huge waste of time!

Intentional Habits of Time

While there are areas of our lives that we have limited control over in the daily-necessities category, there are intentional habits of time we can develop in other areas to work within the time constraints we can't avoid.

Unavoidable time wasters

Waiting for something to happen, traveling to someplace, and communicating with people are unavoidable facets of life. I call these "unavoidable time wasters" because, all too often, we spend too much time doing them, or they can be eliminated, in many cases. The good news is that there are ways to reduce the time used or wasted for these events by reducing the number of times you perform them or by multi-tasking during the event. Some of these times might be:

- Waiting
    - in a reception area for a doctor, hospital visit, or other professional service
    - for your car to be fixed or maintained or for a utility-company service person to show up
    - to board or while riding on a plane, bus, train, or boat
    - for a friend to show up
- Talking
    - on the phone
    - with your neighbor in your driveway for an hour

- Getting stuck in traffic
- Sitting in the jury-duty selection area
- Driving in your car
- Responding to texts and emails

Before I give some examples and suggestions for better uses of your time during these unavoidable lulls, let's state the obvious—constantly being on your cell phone is not usually the most effective use of your time. It's hard to stop looking down every five to ten minutes to check notifications, isn't it? It's a good practice to keep your phone off altogether, or at least on vibrate, and let your calls go directly to voicemail while you are developing intentional habits to use time effectively. Just like email, block out two to three time slots a day to handle the messages you've received. In this way, you can keep your communication with other people as efficient as possible. Also, consider texting people back instead of returning their calls. It takes much less time to send a three-to-four-sentence text than it does to have a fifteen-minute phone conversation. You can help keep track of the time you are spending and remind yourself to put the phone down by utilizing some simple control features already on your cell phone.

Some time wasters are unavoidable, but we have so much control over how we use them. I now look forward to these times because I've developed intentional habits to make the most of them. For example, I had to report to a room at the county courthouse for jury duty and sit around for eight hours while they decided who they were going to select. At least a hundred people were waiting. It amazed me how many of the people in the room completely wasted the entire day just sitting there doing nothing while they were waiting. Ironically, many of them were complaining to each other about how this was a huge waste of their time.

They didn't realize it, but they were the people responsible for wasting their own time. In the entire room, there was only one person who had brought a book with them. I brought my computer, because, at that time, I was writing this book, and I wanted to take advantage of the time I was there. This might sound crazy, but I was looking forward to being locked in the room waiting because I hadn't worked on my book for a couple of weeks. I was excited to have some dedicated time to make progress. I'm growing my wealth every day because this is how I think, plan, and use my time. I think like a rich person, and I value my time.

Life Maintenance
No matter who we are, we all need to take care of certain life-maintenance functions. Things like cooking, grocery shopping, paying bills, mowing the lawn, laundry, and cleaning the house all take time away from the higher-level tasks of improving yourself and making money.

Depending on your financial position, consider how you can outsource or optimize the time it takes to complete life-maintenance tasks. Maybe you can pay another person to shop for your groceries, clean your house, cut your grass, or do your laundry. Do what you can online to avoid standing in unnecessary lines. This may include online banking or ordering common groceries online and getting them delivered. Sometimes you have people in your life who enjoy these kinds of life-maintenance tasks, or you are already paying someone to do similar tasks in other areas of your life. I do not cut grass, shovel snow, or do home repairs. I own income-producing rental properties, and the professionals and contractors I use to maintain those properties also take care of these tasks at my home. Fortunately for me, my wife likes to go grocery shopping and cook. If she did not like to cook and buy groceries, then we would have a personal assistant doing these tasks for us. My administrative assistant pays the bills for my income-producing rental properties and my real-estate brokerage.

ChatGPT and other AI services are an incredible way to save time on repetitive tasks. Whether it's drafting emails or brainstorming content, this AI can handle it, freeing you up to focus on bigger goals. It's like having a reliable virtual assistant at your fingertips. Don't underestimate the power of AI to optimize your day.

When a life-maintenance task arises, I ask myself, *Will it help me increase my knowledge, make money for me, or bring enjoyment to me, or will it help other people?* If not, then I try to hire it out, ask someone else to do it, or avoid it.

Downtime and Entertainment
As humans, we can't work all the time. Sometimes we need to simply relax by ourselves or with our loved ones. Other times, we go to movies, concerts, or restaurants. We spend time on social media or gaming. We spend time pursuing our hobbies and personal interests. Although we all need time to enjoy ourselves, we can still consider whether we are taking too much time for entertainment. The key here is to find the work-life balance that works for you.

Before I changed my mindset about becoming successful, I used to go out every Friday and Saturday night just because it was the weekend—not for any other reason. I just could not stay home on the weekend. I was so afraid I was going to miss something. When I finally realized all that partying was not getting me anywhere, I sat down and figured out how much time and money I was using going out on the weekends. Between getting ready to go out, being out, and recovering from being out late, I was using twenty-five hours a week. I was spending hundreds of dollars every weekend. This motivated me to stay home on the weekends and give up alcohol for a while. To this day, it is one of the biggest positive changes for me. The impact was immediate and profound.

Excessive entertainment time can eat into the hours we have left for personal improvement and growing wealth. The average American spends two to three hours on TV/digital video and three to four hours on social media, with overall Internet usage at close to six and a half hours a day. Gamers spend an average of nearly eight hours a week playing video games. As an experiment, try turning the TV off for one month. Much of the programming isn't very good for your mind, anyway. A lot of video games contain excessive violence, and social media has too much drama. Put the video games and social media aside for thirty days. You will be amazed how you will fill the time you free up with more productive activities.

If you want to free up time to become rich, then stop playing fantasy sports. This is an avoidable time waster you can cut from your life immediately; it won't hurt at all or reduce your quality of life one bit. I don't play fantasy real-estate investing. I do the real thing. I don't play Monopoly. I play the real game of life! Unless all your fantasy-sports-league buddies are more successful than you, then you need to cut this time waster and get serious about becoming rich. If you spend a lot of time playing fantasy sports, then that is what you will be good at.

How you use your leisure time varies from person to person. If you want to focus on becoming rich, then you should start watching how you spend this time. I know I keep coming back to it, but whatever you spend a lot of time doing is what you'll be good at. All of us must spend time doing things that aren't necessarily contributing to growing our wealth and success. However, truly rich people don't waste time if they can avoid it, and they consider everything they do in the context of becoming and staying successful.

Proactive Uses of Time

You may notice that much of our discussion of time is about how we can turn any type of time "waster" into an opportunity for developing your Life Assets, as described in this book. But you don't always need to react to time wasters; you can be proactive in using your time in a way that will help you build wealth and reach your goals.

Socializing

There are times when unfocused socializing can be using up the precious time that we have available. I don't advise hanging out by the work water cooler or coffee pot, the produce section of the grocery store, or your front sidewalk, talking for an hour with neighbors, acquaintances, or co-workers. When I am getting out of my car in my driveway and my neighbor is in front of his house cutting his grass, I always say "Hello," but I keep walking. I have stuff to do if I'm going to be successful. Unless your neighbor is a potential mentor, coach, or lender, then don't hang out discussing politics and the weather for an hour.

Combine socializing with other activities that are important to you. Use social activities to meet and network with new people (see your Life Asset #2: People) by attending a seminar, conference, or mastermind group. If you're looking to build wealth in a particular area, there are likely groups in or near your community that are discussing just that. Can't find these groups locally? No worries—find them online. Start networking by reaching out to key local players in any entrepreneurial field—think real-estate brokers, insurance-company owners, top real-estate agents, successful investors, and leading entrepreneurs. Ask them for their recommendations on groups where you can learn more about your interests and make valuable connections. Find where wealth builders gather, and be there—even if it costs money to join.

Make intentional socializing choices that will prioritize and strengthen the relationships that you value the most: Your family, your closest friends, and others whose presence sustains and supports you. When chosen wisely, these social interactions will also have a positive impact on your health. Many scientific studies have shown connections between strong social bonds and a longer, healthier life.

Self-Education

We will dig into self-education in the next chapter, Life Asset #4: Knowledge, but it is essential to mention it here, as it is a key way to proactively use your time. If you decide to guard your time and change how you live your life, then self-education is the moneymaker. All rich people incorporate self-education into their lives regularly. This is the single biggest change I made to my life that has continually added to my income, wealth, and happiness. You must free up time for this category if you want to change your life and become rich. In fact, this category is why you are trying to free up time in the first place. The more time you spend self-educating, the better your chances are of changing your life and becoming successful in the way that you want.

Forms of self-education include:

- Reading this book
- Meeting with and communicating with your mentor
- Meeting with your Mastermind group
- Attending seminars and conferences
- Reading non-fiction books about self-improvement and investing
- Watching videos and listening to podcasts
- Listening to Audible downloads or audio recordings

I get some of my best self-education done when I'm on a long car ride, or a plane, or otherwise waiting for something else in my life. If you can't afford to buy books on Audible, most public libraries have free audiobooks you can download.

Driving in your car is the perfect time to work on self-education. Most people do nothing with this time; they turn on the radio, use their cell phones to listen to music and news, talk on the phone, or worse, carry on a text conversation. One of the original self-improvement gurus, Jim Rohn, had a term for using your driving time to create self-education. He called this self-education during driving time "Automobile University." Mr. Rohn recommended listening to motivational and educational content when you are driving. I almost never listen to news or music on the radio or my cell phone anymore. I use my cell phone to play Audible books and podcasts of motivational, educational, and wealth-building recordings. I have a whole collection of books on Audible that I play in my car if I am taking longer trips, like the two-hour drive to Pittsburgh to visit my sisters.

There is much more about the value of building your knowledge through self-education in the next chapter on your Life Asset #4: Knowledge. You will find more examples and suggestions there.

Creating Passive Income and Building Wealth
Do you remember the discussion earlier in the book about what it means to be rich? As I stated earlier, you are not rich because you have a lot of money or assets. You acquire income and assets because you think and act like a rich person, living your life with personal and financial freedom. Being rich isn't the result of having money. Having money is the result of thinking and acting rich.

Creating passive income and building wealth is what happens when you spend enough time thinking and acting like a rich person. The beliefs, wisdom, knowledge, and mindset offered in this book will lead you to acquire investments and start businesses that will help you create passive income and build wealth. Examples of things you can do to get to this point would be trading stocks, developing your own online affiliate companies, marketing your services or products, buying an income-producing rental property, selling products or your own expertise online, starting a multi-level marketing company, or selling advertising on your blog, podcast, or YouTube channel.

If you focus on spending as much time as possible implementing the knowledge, beliefs, and concepts from this book, you will eventually own the assets listed above. Whatever you spend a lot of time doing, that is what you will be good at. Spend a lot of time acting rich, and before you know it, you will own assets like the ones above.

Tracking Your Time

It's amazing how little we know about our own habits and actions. We just don't realize how much money, time, or effort we spend on things until we make a conscious effort to track and record the real facts. If your goal is to stop wasting time so you can spend more hours acting like a rich person, then you need to know where all your time is currently going. Do you really know how much time you are spending on your daily activities? You might think you do, but trust me, you have no idea how much time you are wasting until you start writing it down. You track what you are doing, so that you can make the necessary changes to reach your goal. If you don't really know what you are doing, then how can you make the adjustments that lead to success?

Purchase a small journal, and start tracking the time you spend doing things. You can also use the resource below if you need more structure. Do this for sixty days, using the time categories outlined in this chapter, and see where your time is going. If you are like most people, you will need to stop wasting time if you want to spend more time acting like a rich person. You can't free up time if you don't know where your time is going in the first place.

Below is an example of how you could analyze where you're currently using your time. Based on a 24-hour day and 365 days in a year,

THE SIX STEPS TO LASTING WEALTH

we all get 8,760 hours a year to live our lives: 24 hours X 365 days = **8,760 hours**.

- If you sleep 7 hours a night, then you will be sleeping **2,555 hours** per year.

- If you eat 3 meals per day and it takes 30 minutes to eat each meal, then you spend 1.5 hours per day X 365 days = **548 hours** per year eating.

- Let's allow 2 hours per day for hygiene and 3 hours a week for exercise. Let's add 10 hours a year for doctors and dentists. The total time used annually for hygiene and health is:
  (2 hours X 365 days) + (3 hours x 52 weeks) + 10 hours per year = **896 hours** per year.

- If you work 40 hours a week and you receive 2 weeks of vacation time a year from your employer, then you are working 50 weeks out of the year. You will be working at your current source of income for **2,000 hours** a year.

- Let's estimate that unexpected interruptions, emergencies, and accidents use 3 hours a month, so that is **36 hours** per year.

- Let's estimate 1 hour per day for unavoidable time wasters, which covers all the time you spend waiting, traveling, or communicating. 1 hour x 365 days = **365 hours** per year.

- The total time estimated for the Life Maintenance category is 8 hours per week or **416 hours** per year.

- Next, let's estimate some time for socializing and entertainment. If you take 2 vacation weeks a year, that is 14 days x 24 hours = **366 hours** per year.

- If you are married and you have children, let's estimate you spend at least 3 hours a day giving your family love, support, and affection. If you are involved with your kids' sports activities, then this number is probably higher. It is hard for me to attach an accurate time usage to this task because I don't know your family status. The 3 hours also cover socializing with friends, neighbors, co-workers, and relatives. 3 hours x 365 days = **1095 hours** per year.

- The average American spends 2 to 5 hours per day watching TV, using social media, or viewing Internet-based entertainment each day. Let's be optimistic and only use 1 hour per day for this: 1 hour x 365 days = **365 hours** per year.

- I don't know if you like movies at the theatre or if you can afford to eat out at restaurants. I'm sure you have a hobby or personal interest. Let's estimate we all spend an average of 2 hours a week on these time usages: 2 hours per week x 52 weeks = **104 hours** per year.

Below is our grand-total estimate of time used annually to live our lives: 2555+548+896+2000+36+365+416+366+1095+365+104 = **8746 hours per year.**

This estimate of how you live your life is only 14 hours per year less than the 8,760 hours you have available each year. I did not try to make these numbers close. I just estimated the time usage in each category by doing some research online and using my own personal experiences.

Unfortunately, this does not leave much time to change your life through self-education, creating passive income, or wealth building—*unless* you can evaluate and change what you are doing to optimize the time you have.

Putting It Together

You are strengthening your Life Assets #1: Mindset and #2: People. Next on the list is using your time in ways that you choose. Don't let your time control you when you could be controlling it. The motto of this chapter is: Whatever you spend a lot of time doing, that is what you will be good at. Do what you can to claw back minutes or hours on your bare necessities and Life Maintenance tasks so you can create more proactive uses of your time such as intentional socializing, self-education, and passive-income development. You are saving time so you can spend it on more-positive, wealth-building activities.

Strategies to Develop Life Asset #3: Time

This chapter is full of examples and suggestions you can use to develop your Life Asset #3: Time. Here are some key takeaways and activities to get you started *today*:

5 quick things to do right now:

1. Examine your "bare necessity" time obligations. See where you can gain back even an hour of your weekly time.
2. Make a list of your tendencies or habits that are wasting time in your life.
3. Add app time limits on the apps that are wasting your time the most.
4. Automate what you can of your Life Maintenance tasks to free up time for the ways you want to spend your time.
5. Use socializing time more efficiently to make new connections with people who can help encourage your own wealth-building path.

TIME

Extra Credit: Create and write down a system for how you will use unavoidable time wasters that show up daily. What will you do if you have 10 minutes? 30 minutes? 2 hours? Have it on hand so you don't even need to think about what you will do in that time.

Resources for Support

> For more resources on Time Management, visit: *https://www.selfmadewealth.co/Products*

◆ ◆ ◆

LIFE ASSET #4

KNOWLEDGE

"Your formal education will make you a living, but your self-education will make you a fortune."

—Jim Rohn

A *few years ago*, I took a fly-fishing trip to a South Pacific island named Kiritimati. I couldn't wait to take off. Utilizing the Life Assets we've already learned about, I know that what I spend my time on is what I will be good at doing. I prepared to use the sixteen-hour trip to my advantage. I did not have inflight Internet access, so I downloaded three new Audible books onto my cell phone and my computer. I made sure my trip was highly productive and full of education. I wanted to spend as much time as possible developing my mind and acting like a person growing well, so that is what I became good at.

Building my knowledge through self-education isn't something that is difficult for me. In fact, I love and enjoy it. I obsess about it. After learning things, I take massive action. And, yes, my self-education does, indeed, remove me from my comfort zone.

I just can't get enough knowledge. After I finish a twelve-hour day at my company, I go home and watch YouTube videos about wealth building, marketing, social-media techniques, investing, personal improvement, and health. I love seeking knowledge and becoming a better person through that knowledge. I'm in love with constantly evolving and improving. Once when I was out to dinner with my wife and some other couples, I snuck off to the restroom three times to listen to some audio recordings on personal improvement because I was so into what I was hearing. I couldn't put it down. My wife asked me if I was sick because I kept going to the restroom!

This love of learning, self-education, and the pursuit of knowledge is another difference that separates rich people from those with a poverty mindset. Wealthy people understand the direct connection between their success and their self-education. The richest people in the world are the most successful learners. Rich people are always pursuing more knowledge. People who haven't found success often think education is merely a necessary and temporary hoop to jump through just to get a job.

People who have worked toward personal and financial freedom know that the more they learn, the more they earn. They are lifelong learners because they realize their self-education and knowledge are the ways to increase their income and net worth. The wealthiest people in the world block out time regularly to read books, attend seminars and conferences, and pay mentors and coaches to help them learn the skills necessary to grow their wealth. Warren Buffett reads two hours every day. Bill Gates takes a two-week vacation every year to focus on reading books.

Many people view education as a dreaded task or process that they can't wait to complete. Unfortunately, many assume they need to graduate from only high school or college to get a job, and many others haven't even had much education beyond high school. The problem lies in the fact that typical jobs for those with only a high-school diploma don't pay very well. It is getting harder and harder to find a job after graduation from college. These jobs allow you only to trade your time for money, which has limited income potential.

Rich people view education as an investment for their future, not a necessary task. I truly believe the best investment you can ever make is educating yourself. Your mind is the most important asset you own. If you want to become a better person and become financially successful, then you must invest in yourself every chance you get.

If you want to change your life and become rich, you need to be obsessed with changing the way you think, act, and believe through your mindset, the people around you, how you spend time, and by making self-education a passion and a priority. You must tap into and build your Life Asset #4: Knowledge. You must fall in love with lifelong education.

A Lifelong Pursuit

Self-education isn't a one-time task; it's an ongoing lifestyle for achieving wealth and success. Think of it like nurturing a plant with sunlight and water. If you keep feeding your mind with knowledge, your income and net worth will keep growing, and you'll change your life for the better. Rich people see education as a thrilling investment, eagerly reading books and attending seminars. They understand that lifelong learning is key to wealth.

Becoming rich isn't achieved through a single podcast or video; it's a lifelong journey of self-education and personal growth, similar to maintaining a healthy body. Staying wealthy requires a commitment to continuous learning, and it brings daily motivation to succeed. Take self-improvement author John Maxwell. His perspective is that, if he focuses on personal improvement and education, he can't help but accomplish all his goals. His goals keep coming automatically because he is always growing as a person and a professional. If your life is not where you want it, and it has not grown or changed for a long time, it is because you have not changed as a person. Your inability to change is caused by your lack of continued education. You are lacking personal development. If you don't pursue personal development throughout your life, then your emotional, social, professional, and financial growth will stop.

Not everyone finds traditional school easy, enjoyable, or even useful, so you may need to go back to Asset #1: Mindset in order to keep you motivated and remind you of the long-term goal of building lasting wealth. Stop viewing education as a burden or a task. Rich people view education as a fun investment they are passionate about. Rich people can't wait to start reading the next book or listening to the next podcast or webinar. I always have my next book on my desk waiting to be read before I am finished with the book I am currently reading. I am always stoked whenever I have another seminar or conference in my schedule. I have become a self-education junkie because I have learned how my self-education is the fuel that is growing my life in incredible ways. The more I learn, the more I earn.

Formal Education vs. Self-education

Formal education is designed to teach you specific skills, so that you can find a job in fields like factories, restaurants, offices, healthcare, or engineering. This includes grade school, middle school, high school, vocational schools, and college, where you earn degrees or certificates to show you've finished the program and can qualify for jobs. These programs usually have set schedules and locations, although many are now available online. Most people complete these education stages because they're necessary for finding a job, often counting down the days until they're done.

Your self-education, on the other hand, can come from many sources and typically revolves around personal, health, or financial improvement. You never finish your self-education like you do a formal education program. You don't get a degree or certificate that helps you apply for jobs. Self-education is not mandatory and is pursued only if someone is passionate about changing their life and growing as a person. There are no set times or dates for this education.

We live in a time with more abundance and opportunity than ever in the history of the world. In the past, you had to learn from your parents or your formal education. Today, millions of people are online sharing their knowledge, beliefs, and skills. Leveraging other people's knowledge is one of the fastest and most efficient ways to change your life and learn quickly. Udacity, Udemy, Skillshare, and YouTube are popular online platforms today for both free and paid life-changing education.

Popular self-education and personal-improvement topics cover just about everything. You can learn how to:

- Develop a positive attitude
- Sleep better at night
- Remove stress from your life
- Embrace a better diet
- Start your own business
- Invest in real estate or stocks
- Get out of debt
- Find people to lend you money
- Maximize your social-media skills
- Market your business
- Negotiate and communicate
- Set goals and plan

- Begin a multi-level marketing business
- Start your own YouTube channel
- Start your own podcast

Accessing the School of Wealth

"The School of Wealth" is a phrase I coined to refer to an invisible club or society that rich people have access to that others do not. You don't get a degree from it, and it is not a brick-and-mortar building. This is how The School of Wealth works. Most people have never been taught how to properly earn enough money, keep it, and use it effectively during their lifetime. You see, formal education may affect how much earned income you make in a salaried or hourly job, but it has nothing to do with real financial independence.

Most people spend thirteen to twenty years going to school to learn how to earn money at a job, but they spend little or no time teaching themselves how to keep and grow what they earn. They don't learn how to make their money work for them. After they get a job, they stop educating themselves completely. They don't learn how to think like rich people and let their money work for them. But those who have acquired wealth are all well-educated in the art of making, growing, and retaining money. This education was not acquired through a conventional school or university; it was acquired at . . . you guessed it. The School of Wealth.

Our public-education system was designed to prepare individuals for employment rather than for personal and financial freedom. The School of Wealth is where individuals interested in building wealth learn about wealth and how to attain it. Scholars at The School of Wealth often surround themselves with already-wealthy individuals, including family, friends, colleagues, and mentors they meet at seminars and conferences.

If you're like most people, you may not have had the opportunity to be exposed to those who understand wealth principles. If your family and social circle lacked an abundance mindset, you may have grown up with a scarcity mentality. In the past, individuals with such mindsets had limited access to those with wealth mindsets and couldn't benefit from The School of Wealth.

But in the time we live in, everyone has access. With the beliefs, knowledge, and principles in this book and others like it, as well as the amazing opportunities that the Internet has created, the doors to The School of Wealth are now wide open to you. And, best of all, the tuition is free! In our world of technology, you have access to many amazing people who are waiting to help you change your life for the better. You now have the same opportunity and education available to you as everyone else.

Making Time for Self-education

To make self-education work for you, you will need to stop wasting time and make a plan. You absolutely can fit it into your schedule, but it is also easy to put off. Live your life around your self-education, not the other way around.

If you commit to reading just 10 pages of a book every day, you'll finish a 300-page book in a month. That's 12 books a year, which is more than enough to be continually absorbing new knowledge, especially if you're choosing the right books. But don't stop there; layer in a daily dose of educational YouTube videos or online courses, and you're not just double-dipping—you're accelerating your growth. Ten to fifteen minutes a day watching videos in your field, or focusing on a skill you're looking to master, can make a dramatic difference over time. Do this, and you're not just outpacing the crowd; you're lapping them. You'll easily land in the top 10 percent of learners, continually fortifying your personal and professional life.

The Education Quiz

Jim Rohn tells a story from a time when he was not yet the great personal-improvement guru he has become today. At the time of the clip, Jim was not doing well in life. He was broke. His life had not changed or improved in more than five years. He had just met his first mentor, who asked him the following questions: How many books have you read in the past month? How many seminars have you attended in the past three months? How much money have you saved in the past year? Jim's answer to all these questions was "None."

This story illustrates the fact that, because Jim had not changed his life, his income and savings had not changed, either. His mentor was telling him that he needed to change if he wanted his money or job status to improve. Self-education is the number-one way you can change. Changing yourself is what becoming successful is all about. Use these questions to assess where your knowledge about wealth and success-building is today. Ask yourself the following questions:

- How many non-fiction books have you read in the past year?
- How many seminars or conferences have you attended in the past year?
- When was the last time your formal educational level increased?
- How many YouTube videos about investing, business, or entrepreneurship have you watched in the past month?
- Whose podcasts are you currently listening to?
- Do you have any written goals?
- How much has your income increased over the past five years?
- How much money do you have in savings?

- How much money do you have in retirement accounts?
- If you lose your job tomorrow, can you still pay your bills?
- Is your credit score more than 700?

Putting It Together

Long-term development takes a long-term commitment to self-education. Once you've focused and committed your Life Asset #1: Mindset to that path, developing your Life Asset #4: Knowledge will allow you to be at the top of your game—nimble and adaptable in an ever-changing wealth-building game. While formal education can develop your skills, your real asset is your ability to self-educate. Use the plethora of resources available through books, seminars, podcasts, and videos to stay current and build your knowledge. Don't forget the knowledge to be found through the people you know and the professional networks you have cultivated. Many resources are free, but there is also much to be gained from paid resources and networks.

Strategies to Develop Life Asset #4: Knowledge

This chapter is full of examples and suggestions you can use to develop your Life Asset #4: Knowledge. Here are some key takeaways and activities to get you started *today*:

5 quick things to do right now:

1. Make sure you read this book completely and follow its advice and habits, including following the YouTube and podcast channels from the teachers I've mentioned.

2. Read one specific book that teaches you how to improve your life.

3. Subscribe and download an audiobook app on your phone, like Audible.

4. Attend a live seminar that teaches something you are passionate about.

5. Join a club or group of people who are enthusiastic about your goals.

Extra Credit: Stop or reduce your time watching TV and sports on TV, or using social media for entertainment.

◆ ◆ ◆

LIFE ASSET #5

MONEY

*"Money isn't everything,
but it's right up there with oxygen."*

—Zig Ziglar

One of the most painful memories I have is when my brother died at the age of 30. It was extremely painful to lose my brother at such a young age. This loss for my family and me was compounded by the fact that we were not by his side when he passed away. My brother was living in Washington, DC, and we knew he was very ill. He had just been rushed to the hospital and was not given long to live. My parents were struggling financially at that time. Because of our financial situation, we could not just hop on a plane or jump in a car and rush to him. We had one older, run-down car, and it would not make the trip to be with him. Before we could figure out how to get to Washington, he died alone in a hospital bed without us by his side.

I can't explain to you the feeling of helplessness my family experienced that day, all because of the lack of money. I can't, I won't forget that experience, and I've vowed never to let myself or my family be poor again. I refuse to ever live paycheck-to-paycheck again or be in a position where I can't be there for my family in a time of need.

I have been poor, and I have been financially free. I will choose financial freedom over being poor any day. I had my days when I was scraping coins out of my car seat to buy another gallon of gas. When I was in college, I hitchhiked back and forth from Rochester, New York, to Erie, Pennsylvania, to visit my family on the weekends. Today is so much different. I've been able to harness my Life Asset #5: Money and make it work for me. It can work for you, too.

Although popular media would like you to believe that the American dream is dead, I don't believe it is. It is true that the old way of working the same job for 30 years and retiring with a pension has gone away. This financial model has been replaced with an entirely new set of opportunities and abundance: a new American dream.

For me, it means I can quit my job to do what I want, when and where I want. It means I will have passive income from my assets and investments that will support my ideal standard of living and allow me to continue to grow my income and net worth. My ideal American dream includes having the time and money to help other people, owning my home free and clear of debt, being able to take vacations when I want, having multiple sources of passive income, and having adequate health and life insurance. I can maintain my standard of living even if I quit my job—or, if my life partner or I get sick, we can still pay our bills. The American dream means I have great credit, I am debt-free, and I have cash in the bank.

Today the middle class and the lifestyle of being an employee are under siege and may be dying a slow death. We now have a demographic in our society that the media refers to as the "Working Poor." This is a sector of our society that works for money but lives in poverty because their income is barely enough to live on. The middle class and this working-poor class are becoming poorer each day because their income never goes up, but the cost of food, housing, transportation, insurance, education, and healthcare continue to rise every year. The next ten to fifteen years are going to usher in some amazing technological advancements such as robots, automation, and artificial intelligence. It remains to be seen how this will affect employees from the middle class and working poor, but most predictions are that 30–40 percent of all jobs performed by humans will be gone. It is more important than ever to learn how to think like a rich person if you want not only to *survive* financially but also to *prosper and grow* toward personal and financial independence.

This dream is an achievable lifestyle for anyone who knows where to find it. By combining hard work, intelligence, and providing value to others, you can lead an exceptional life marked by financial independence. In order to do this, you need to be willing to take control of your finances.

Eight Steps to a Better Financial Future

The good news is that we are living longer. The not-so-good news is that, with that longevity and a quickly evolving job market, we need more money to support our additional years. Most of us can still improve our financial literacy and get more serious about Life Asset #5: Money.

I will be honest with you, though—it isn't always easy to change your finances. Change of any kind isn't easy. Almost anything worth having in life requires effort and change. I look at it this way: if you are broke and struggling financially, you are probably suffering. So, if you're suffering anyway, why not suffer to make your life better? Why not suffer and sacrifice to have the life you desire? I have made those sacrifices and put in the work, and, now, I am realizing the new American dream every day. Life is good for me, and it can be for you, too, if you want it. It is doable for everyone.

The Internet is full of great ideas for strengthening your financial future, but this book boils it down to eight "must-do's." Below is a list

THE SIX STEPS TO LASTING WEALTH

of changes every person should make if they want to pursue financial freedom and achieve the American dream. The following steps will set you on a path to either turn your financial future around or strengthen and accelerate your journey:

1. Get lean and mean.
2. Start practicing delayed gratification.
3. Maximize your current income.
4. Get out of debt.
5. Fix your credit.
6. Get educated about how money works.
7. Save 5–10 percent of everything you earn.
8. Create a personal financial statement.

Step 1: Get Lean and Mean

Cutting unnecessary spending, getting out of debt, and saving money alone will not make you personally and financially free. Building wealth always goes back to your Life Asset #1: Mindset. Becoming rich is about changing the way you think, what you believe, how you make decisions, and who you surround yourself with. But once you understand and begin to act, think, and believe like a rich person, you are going to need money to start investing in yourself and in cashflow-producing assets.

Wealth-building people are rich because they guard their money. They spend money only on things that bring value to their life. They spend money on the essentials, such as having a comfortable home to live in, transportation, food, and healthcare. They also spend money on education and investments. I'm not saying rich people don't splurge and buy nice homes, luxury cars, or vacations, but they do that only after they have a comfortable cushion of wealth.

If you want to change your life and become rich, then stop spending money on anything unless you absolutely need it. You must pay your mortgage or your rent, or you won't have a roof over your head. You must make your car payments and put gas in your car, or you won't be able to get to work. You need food. You must pay your electric and gas bills, so you can have lights and heat in your home. These expenses are unavoidable.

When I talk about giving things up, I'm talking about relinquishing things you can live without. The operative phrase here is "things you can live without." You can't live without food, but you can live without alcohol. You can't live without a roof over your head, but you can live without gambling. You can't live without heat and lights in your home, but you can live without cable TV. You can't live without food, but you can stop eating out at expensive restaurants and buying expensive coffee. There is a never-ending list of things we all spend money on that can be put off for a while—or even eliminated altogether. If you are serious about changing your life and building wealth, you will need to delay spending money on things you can live without.

Step 2: Start Practicing Delayed Gratification

If you want to change your life and become rich, then you need to embrace the concept of delayed gratification. I am proposing living lean and mean only until you get to a place in life where you can afford to take all the vacations and drink all the Starbucks coffee you want. Below is the definition of "Delayed Gratification" from Wikipedia.

> "Delayed gratification, or deferred gratification, describes the process that the subject undergoes when the subject resists the

temptation of an immediate reward in preference for a later reward. Generally, delayed gratification is associated with resisting a smaller but more immediate reward to receive a larger or more-enduring reward later. A growing body of literature has linked the ability to delay gratification to a host of other positive outcomes, including academic success, physical health, psychological health, social competence, and financial freedom."

Many of us have a problem waiting for things and sacrificing our immediate gratification in the short term in order to enjoy long-term rewards. Taking control of your life and making sacrifices has a positive effect on us. Our confidence and self-esteem grow when we gain that sense of control. Accepting and practicing delayed gratification is critical for supporting the change needed to become a successful, wealth-building person. Waiting for things is good for you both mentally and emotionally.

We all make purchases we could live without. Stop eating at restaurants and coffee shops. Start buying groceries, cooking at home, and bagging your lunch. You will save money and eat healthier, too. Give up popular, convenient chain restaurants that sell overpriced products. Six-dollar coffees at one place are generally no better than a $2 coffee at the convenience store.

Try not to buy any new clothing unless you absolutely need it. Keep wearing your clothes until they're worn out or no longer fit. If your car is paid off and runs fine, then keep it until it doesn't get you to where you need to go. Don't buy a car just because the one you have isn't flashy and new anymore. If you must buy a car, then buy a used one. New cars are a huge waste of money and depreciate the moment you drive them off the lot.

Try to resist buying toys and clothes for your pets. Pets need food, water, and love. I don't know about your dogs, but mine just destroy any toys we give them within a couple of days anyway. It is like throwing money in the garbage can.

Let's talk about cell phones, cable TV, Netflix, and Sirius radio subscriptions. These technology services cost you a ton of money every month. It might be worth considering reducing your cell-phone plan. Unless you use your phone for work, maybe you can reduce your plan to save money. You might not need a huge data plan for your phone unless you use it for work. If you find yourself using a lot of data on your phone merely for entertainment purposes, then shut it off.

Personally, I'm not a big fan of most TV programming. Many of the newer shows startle me with their negativity and violence. I'm sure there are good shows out there, but I prefer to just watch YouTube videos that help me improve my life and educate me. You are the only person who can ultimately decide how important this stuff is to you. But if you're spending a lot of money on technology only for entertainment purposes, it might be worth considering paring down your bills by getting rid of cable or Netflix, at least for a short time. Not only will you save money, but this is a great way to free up time to add self-education to your life.

I don't know how you feel about sharing your living space with another person, but renting your extra rooms to a roommate is a fantastic way to get some extra needed cash flow to pay down debt or invest in yourself. If you have an apartment, consider getting a roommate. If you own a home, consider renting your spare bedrooms through a company like Airbnb.

Let's talk about transportation. If you and your life partner each own a car, you could consider going down to one car. Before you call me crazy, give it some consideration. Many of us drive our car to work, where it sits for 8–10 hours in our employer's parking lot. If you or your partner have employment scenarios that do not require a car to perform your work, then it is very realistic to live with one car. Let's say your car payment is around $400, with about $300 spent monthly for car insurance, repairs, and fuel. That's $700 a month. What if you could share a car with your partner or even another person? For twelve months, the savings would be $8,400. What a fantastic way to free up money to pay off a credit card, start an emergency fund, or start a new business! Twelve months is not that long a period, and you can reap so many benefits.

We all spend money on personal grooming products and services to help us look beautiful. Consider whether you really need to pay $20–30 for a bottle of shampoo, or would a $10 product work just as well? Once at a party, a guy I met told me he cuts his own hair. He was the best-looking guy at the party, and his hair looked great. Stop paying salons to trim and paint your nails. Do it yourself for a while so you can save money and pay down your bills. It's great to splurge occasionally on these things, but it is better to practice delayed gratification and wait until you get out of debt.

In my opinion, extended families today spend way too much money at Christmas time. Ask your parents, friends, and siblings to skip buying retail gifts for each other for one year so you all can save some money. Come up with another idea to help reduce the money you spend at this expensive time of year. You could each exchange some used personal items as gifts. How about giving each other homemade food or baked goods? Maybe all of you can agree to make something from scratch for each other. Do something other than going to all the big-box stores and running up your credit cards.

Alcohol, recreational drugs, and gambling—not only is this stuff a waste of your money, it is not good for your health or your family's future. You will also be surrounding yourself with other people who need these vices—probably not good company for you, anyway. If you won't or can't remove these vices from your life, it will be very hard to become rich. Abusing drugs and alcohol will keep you poor. If you have an addiction, do everything you can to find the help you need to turn your life around. It will be very hard to leave poverty behind if you have addiction problems.

I know giving up cigarettes is one of the hardest vices to quit. Nicotine is a very addictive substance. We all know how bad cigarettes are for our physical health, but also consider how damaging they are to your financial health. Below is an analysis of what you are giving up financially to be a lifelong smoker. If you pay an average of $10 for a pack of cigarettes over the next forty years and you smoke four packs a week, then you'll spend about $2,080 per year. If you invested that $2,080 each year into a mutual fund that paid just a 5 percent annual return on your money, after forty years, you would have a mutual fund worth $251,264! Do you know how many rental properties you could buy, businesses you could start, or investments you could make with that money?

In general, analyze where you splurge daily, weekly, or monthly on luxury products that could be put off temporarily or for the long term. Consider delaying the items and activities that are not truly helping you reach your goals or improving your well-being.

Step 3: Maximize Your Current Income

There are only two ways to take control of your finances. You can reduce the amount of money you spend through cutting and delaying, or you can increase the amount of money you bring in. For the short term, let's make sure you are maximizing your income for your current level of education and expertise. Right now, our goal is to make sure you are getting all the income possible from your current employment or investments. Once you get control of your financial life, you can start to prepare for making investments in your career, real estate, or business idea.

Ask yourself the following five questions:

- When was the last time your employer gave you a raise?
- When was the last time you asked your employer for a raise?

When was the last time you received a promotion?

When was the last time you asked for a promotion?

When was the last time you updated your resume and tried to find a higher-paying job?

According to a Career Builder survey, 56 percent of workers fail to negotiate a better salary. More than half of workers indicated they feel uncomfortable asking for more money. I am a firm believer in the age-old phrase *Ask and you shall receive*. If you don't ask for more money or a promotion, then you probably won't get it. Start asking your employer for more responsibility and more money. It might be uncomfortable, but uncomfortability is part of being human, and you will learn and grow from the experience, no matter the outcome.

If your employer does not consider your request, then maybe it's time to move on and up. Get your resume updated, and start applying for better-paying jobs. If you receive a better job offer, you can always go back to your current employer and give them the opportunity to match the higher pay. If they don't match it, then maybe it's time to move on to a new opportunity.

Step 4: Get Out of Debt

In order to secure a healthier financial future, you need to get out of debt. This section is a very high-level summary. Reading books by Suze Orman and Dave Ramsey will give you the micro-details for a complete study of this goal. For now, I want to impress upon you the importance of getting out of debt and how it relates to becoming rich. Dave Ramsey said it best: Your earned income is your best wealth-building tool. This wealth-building tool will not be available to you if you are living paycheck to paycheck because of all your debt.

Trying to become wealthy is like running in a race. Too much debt is like a ball and chain tied to your ankle. Can you imagine how hard it is to run in a race when you have a ball and chain around your ankle? You won't get too far.

Your depth of debt is directly connected to your credit score. I can tell you from experience that, if you are in debt and have poor credit, it will be difficult to invest money in assets like real estate, stocks, mutual funds, or your own business. You need good credit and access to some of your earned income if you want to start acquiring cashflow-producing assets or start a business. I have read many books and heard numerous so-called gurus talk about becoming financially free and rich even if you have no money, credit, time, or experience. If this were true, then everyone would be rich. In my world, it takes time, hard work, self-education, good credit, and access to money.

Below is a simple plan that has been used by millions of people to eliminate bad debt.

- **Stop using any form of credit immediately.**

This should be something you do for good. Credit cards are not money. Credit cards are financial poison. If you don't have the money, then don't buy the item. It's that simple. If you must use a credit card to buy something, then you can't afford it.

- **Make a list of the balances you owe for all your debts and the monthly payment for each debt.**

Don't include things like heating and electric bills or groceries, which are recurring expenses you can't live without. These expenses are not debt. Instead, forms of debt include car payments, credit cards, store charge accounts, student loans, family loans, outstanding medical bills, home-mortgage payments, and home-equity lines of credit. When you make your list of the balances you owe, include the name of the creditor, the interest rate, your balance owed, the minimum monthly payment due, and any extra payment amount you can commit to making.

It is important to make this list in writing. If you want to accomplish a goal, it must be clearly defined and written down. Also, by writing down your plan and goal, you'll start to make it more obtainable. Below is an example of a debt tracker I made in MS Excel. If you go to your cell-phone-app store, there are numerous budgeting and debt-reducing applications you can download for free.

NAME	TYPE	BALANCE	RATE	MINIMUM PAYMENT	EXTRA PAYMENT
Jones department store	Store Card	$456.76	21.000%	$15.60	$100.00
Discover	Credit Card	$2,345.67	20.000%	$56.79	
PA Loan System	Student Loan	$4,350.00	2.500%	$175.00	
Mazda Financial	Car Loan	$4,567.89	3.500%	$355.00	
Master Card	Credit Card	$6,578.21	14.000%	$87.89	
Student Loans of America	Student Loan	$8,907.00	3.500%	$250.00	
Bank of Someplace	Home Equity Loan	$13,450.00	3.500%	$132.42	
Bank of Someplace	Home Mortgage	$73,459.09	4.875%	$879.64	

NOTE: Home Mortgage balance includes only principal balance of the loan.
It does not include interest or escrows for real-estate taxes and home insurance.

- **Call all your creditors, and try to get the interest rates lowered.**

Tell them that if they won't lower the rates, then you are going to pay off the entire balance and close the account. Most creditors don't want you to pay off the debt because that is how they make money from you—by charging you a lot of interest.

- **Get a consolidation loan with a lower interest rate to pay off several of your debts that have higher interest rates.**

If you have some equity in your home, a Home Equity Line of Credit (HELOC) is a great way to consolidate debts. The interest rates are typically lower than the rates you are paying on credit cards, store charges, and car loans, and you can write off the interest portion of your payment on your tax return.

- **Make sure you are always paying at least the minimum payment on time for each debt to avoid surcharges and penalties.**

Late payments will also keep you from improving your credit score.

- **Use all extra available cash you can afford to pay down the loan with the smallest balance.**

After this loan has been paid off, then move all extra available money to the loan with the next smallest balance. Keep doing this until you eliminate all bad debt.

Getting out of debt is a critical step toward taking control of your finances and building wealth. Rich people use debt only to make more money—they don't use debt to buy things. When I am talking about getting out of debt, I am talking about eliminating the bad debt from your life, like credit cards. Getting out of debt will improve your credit score, which will help you get loans to buy investments or start a business. But there are other benefits as well—getting out of debt reduces stress, which, in turn, leads to better health. If you want to change your life and have personal and financial freedom, it requires money to invest, start a business, and pay for certain forms of education.

Step 5: Fix Your Credit

We have all made mistakes that have messed up our credit score. Maybe you have missed a payment, opened too many credit-based accounts at once, or over-utilized your available credit. We have all been there, but you can change your credit score. Improving your credit score is critical when you are ready to start acquiring cashflow-producing assets or starting a business. There will be times when you will borrow money to make these acquisitions, and your credit score is an important factor in obtaining this financing. If your credit score is good, you will also receive lower interest rates and lower insurance premiums.

Fixing your credit is a process. Follow these suggestions to improve your credit.

- **Go online, and get a free copy of your credit history and score.**

It is important to know where you stand before you start your journey toward financial freedom. The Fair Credit Reporting Act allows you to obtain free copies of your credit reports from the three credit bureaus: Experian, Equifax, and TransUnion, once a year. You can access these free reports from AnnualCreditReport.com. You can also get your reports directly from Experian, Equifax, and TransUnion. It is important to see your report from each of the three credit bureaus, because your credit report can differ with each one.

- **Fix or remove any errors in the three reports.**

Do this even if you haven't done the work to raise your credit score. You can go to the websites of each of the three credit bureaus to find the instructions on how to fix any errors. You can also hire a credit-repair service to determine if anything on your credit report can be removed or adjusted to help your credit score. Every time you pay off a debt, make sure it is reflected on each of the credit bureaus' reports.

Step 6: Get Educated about How Money Works

When we learned about our Life Asset #4: Knowledge, I talked about becoming a lifelong learner. You can become rich only if you increase the value you bring to other people. You can do this only through a lifelong pursuit of self-education. You need to constantly teach yourself about money: how to earn it, save it, borrow it, invest it, and make it grow for you.

Instead of sitting around watching TV, surfing the Internet, or wasting time on social media, try watching YouTube videos about money, investing, business, and building wealth. Watch videos and read books by Dave Ramsey and Suze Orman. These two money gurus are two of the best in the world for learning about how to get out of debt and how to manage your money.

It amazes me how people will take golf or tennis lessons, but they don't even think of taking money lessons. How many of us have a money coach? We have a dentist, a doctor, and an insurance agent, but most of us never sit down and talk to a financial-services professional. We love to read books like *The Lord of the Rings* and *Fifty Shades of Grey*. How many books on wealth building and investing do you read each year? We enjoy going to ethnic festivals for their food, music, and culture. When was the last time you attended a seminar or conference on financial freedom, investing, or personal improvement? We love watching fictional people live their lives on TV shows. When was the last time you watched a show, movie, or YouTube video that will help you improve your own, real life?

Step 7: Save 5–10 Percent of Everything You Earn

If you are not saving any money, this is something you need to change immediately. I know you might be wondering how you can do this if you are living paycheck to paycheck. Look at it this way. If your paycheck was reduced by 5 percent tomorrow, you would have no choice but to live off 5 percent less money. This is the way you need to approach saving money.

If you read any book about personal finance and money management, they all contain the following statement: Pay yourself first. Open a savings account immediately, and pay yourself first, depositing 5 percent off the top of everything you earn. Use this account only to save money and for nothing else. This is a fund you never touch. As soon as you get paid, deposit 5 percent of your take-home pay in this account. Whatever you have left after you set aside your savings is what you live on. Pay all your mandatory bills next—these are the things you can't live without, like rent money, car payment, groceries, healthcare, and heating and electric bills.

Step 8: Create a Personal Financial Statement

Once you have begun steps 1–7, assess where you are by creating a Personal Financial Statement.

Take the Financial Fitness Quiz

When I was working in the corporate world as an electrical engineer, I heard a statement about companies that now applies to the individual as well. "You either grow, or you die." As harsh as that sounds, the days of performing the same job for 30 years and getting your pension or Social Security check are over. The household and per capita income of middle-class employees has not grown. It has shrunk over the past 100 years, due to corporate greed and overpaid CEOs. Social Security income is projected to be reduced by as much as 25 percent by the United States federal government. With this new wave of technology impacting every aspect of your lives, I believe the middle class is going to take another hit. Now is the time to circle your financial wagons.

Before you begin to implement some of the practices in this chapter, do a checkup on your financial fitness. These questions will assess your current and future financial status:

- Has your annual income increased at least 3.5 percent a year over the past five years?
- Are you saving at least 10 percent of your take-home pay every month?
- If you lose your job tomorrow, can you still pay all your bills?
- If your furnace breaks down tomorrow, can you pay an estimated $2,500 for a new one without using a credit card or another form of debt, or asking a family member for a loan?
- If you or your partner pass away tomorrow, can your family continue to pay all the bills and provide a proper burial?
- If you or your partner pass away tomorrow, do you have enough life insurance to replace their income?
- Have you updated your Personal Financial Statement within the past 12 months?
- If the industry in which you are currently employed becomes obsolete tomorrow, do you have a backup plan for pursuing the same amount of income doing something else?
- Do you have a liquid-cash emergency fund equal to six months of your take-home pay?
- When you reach age 67, will your retirement plan pay you at least 75 percent of your current annual income until you reach the age of ninety?

- Is your credit score 700 or higher?

- Do you have a Last Will and Testament, Power of Attorney, Living Will, and Healthcare Power of Attorney?

If you answered *No* to more than half of these questions, then you need to get serious about your financial future.

Putting It Together

Depending on your financial situation, you might feel that your Life Asset #5: Money is not working for you at the moment, but the good news is that it can be. Take the time to honestly evaluate and reflect (without guilt or regret) about your current financial situation. Then work through the steps to make changes: cut expenses where you can, delay unnecessary purchases, find ways to maximize what you earn from your current job and skill, get out of debt, work on fixing your credit, gain knowledge about making better financial decisions, start saving more money, and make a current Personal Financial Statement. Money flows to people who take care of it, treat it with care, and do good things with it. Money wants to be respected, valued, taken care of, and used to benefit others. It will flow in abundance to those who use it to do the right thing. It might seem impossible, but it is within reach. Harness your Life Asset #5: Money today.

Strategies to Develop Your Life Asset #5: Money

In this chapter, you have found numerous practical suggestions designed to help you enhance your Life Asset #5: Money. Below are some actionable activities that you can begin right away:

MONEY

5 quick things to do right now:

1. Take the Financial Fitness Quiz, and reflect on your results
2. Cut out one extra expense this week.
3. Get a *free* copy of your credit report so you can work on improving it.
4. Set up an automatic transfer that will move 5–10 percent of your income to a savings account.
5. If you haven't yet, take advantage of The Money Playbook, which focuses on your Life Asset #1: Mindset and your wealth-building dreams.

Extra Credit: Make a plan to ask your boss for a raise or a promotion.

Resources for Support

For more resources on MONEY, visit:
https://www.selfmadewealth.co/resources

◆ ◆ ◆

LIFE ASSET #6

HEALTH

*"It is health that is real wealth
and not the pieces of gold and silver."*

—Mahatma Gandhi

I *have played sports my entire life*, and I still play competitive tennis. At one time a few years back, however, I almost stopped playing. I'd found myself struggling every time I played, getting completely winded within twenty minutes, with sweat pouring off my body. I had plantar fasciitis in both feet, an inflamed rotator cuff, tennis elbow, and arthritis in my wrist. Beyond the tennis court, I was completely exhausted by 5 p.m. every day. I had trouble putting in an eight-hour workday and would arrive home exhausted, crashing on the couch.

I assumed it was just my age catching up with me, and I thought maybe it was time to give up competitive sports. In hindsight, that would have been a terrible decision. Instead, I focused on my health and improved my condition to make me healthier and happier today.

Maintaining your Life Asset #6: Health is fundamental to getting rich and realizing your dream life. Without your health, you won't be able to pursue the other Life Assets with gusto. Without good health, you can't leverage your other superpowers. Without your physical and mental health, you might not have the energy to do any of the other strategies that will build wealth for you and the ones you love.

Entire books have been written about diet, exercise, and emotional health. This one chapter alone cannot do justice to these important topics, but this book would be incomplete in helping you if I did not at least discuss my own lessons regarding good health. My health has been instrumental in my own pursuit of financial freedom. Success and good health go together.

I am not a medical doctor, so my advice is based only on my experience and self-education, not the extensive scientific research that your personal medical professional has access to. You are responsible for making decisions about your own health, but in sharing my own journey, I hope it will inspire you to take control of your own.

Look at the best professional athletes in the world—they treat their minds and bodies like temples. When they step on the playing field, they want to deliver peak performance. Your life is no different from theirs. You might think that trying to become rich has nothing to do with physical stamina, but it does. Your physical and mental stamina will be critical if you want to go from being poor to being rich. If you want to become rich, you must have the physical and mental state of a great athlete. Changing your life and becoming rich will be challenging. At times, it will be mentally and physically exhausting.

Becoming rich and pursuing change requires:

- Being motivated
- Having energy throughout the day
- Staying focused
- Having a positive attitude

- Working extra hours
- Being creative
- Avoiding illness
- Committing to change and sacrifice

You can see how good health (or bad health) will influence your other Life Assets. If you are exhausted because you have a poor diet and sleep habits, then you are not going to want to make the sacrifices and put in the time it takes to change. You will have a negative attitude and zero motivation. You won't get up early to read, study, exercise, or pursue goals. You will be tired, and you'll just keep putting off working on your goals until the next day.

What Is Good Health?

Even though most people have different experiences around health, there are some common characteristics of what "good health" entails. I am not a nutritionist, physician, or personal trainer, but I have played sports my entire life, worked out in gyms, and continue to play competitive tennis. Even though I've had many healthy periods in my life, I have also experienced what a poor diet, no exercise, and poison can do to my mind and body. I've lived both ways, and I can definitively say that living healthy is better and more effective to living a successful life. Some of the most important habits and traits that lead to good health are:

- Good-quality sleep
- Proper diet
- Regular hydration
- Regular exercise

- Avoiding stress and toxic people
- Avoiding poisons

If you can improve these areas in your life, you'll feel and look better. Every day, your health will get better, which will only increase your chances of changing your life to become rich.

Quality Sleep

Sleep is critical to strengthening your health, so that you have the energy to make wealth-building changes in your life. Sleep is the way your mind and body recharge and repair themselves. Your brain and body are like cell-phone batteries. You recharge your entire being with a good night of sleep.

Lack of sleep or chronic insomnia can be debilitating. Insomnia causes employers billions of dollars in lost productivity every year as well as numerous health problems. About ten years ago, I was exiting an eight-year relationship with a girlfriend, and my business partnership was starting down the road of what would become a three-year business divorce. The stress from these events was tremendous. I could not sleep more than a couple of hours a night. I had chronic insomnia. I was barely able to keep my full-time job. I had hives all over my body, constant nosebleeds, terrible cramps in my feet and legs, and even dental problems. The stress was ruining my life. Eventually, I moved on emotionally from these stressful events, but it was still another year before my sleep returned to normal levels. I know what a lack of sleep can do to a person. Without sleep, both your focus and your commitment to change your life go right out the window.

When I get eight hours of quality sleep, my productivity and creativity the next day are noticeably improved. I spend more time writing books

HEALTH

and creating seminars. I spend more time working on real-estate deals. I am happy all day long. If someone told me that, for a $10,000 annual fee, I could be guaranteed eight hours of uninterrupted sleep every night, I would gladly pay that fee. I know I would make the $10,000 back several times every year with my increased productivity and creativity.

For me, exceptional sleep means sleeping at least seven hours per night without tossing and turning or lying awake for hours at a time. I'm not a sleep therapist, but I have discovered some tips that might help you consistently have a good night's sleep:

- **Make sure you are sleeping in a cool, dark, and quiet bedroom.** Studies show that you will sleep better under these conditions. Also, go to bed and wake up at the same time as much as possible. Going to bed at the same time every night and waking up at the same time every morning will reset your sleep clock, and you will start to fall asleep more easily and stay asleep longer.

- **If you go to bed and you can't fall asleep, don't lie there tossing and turning.** You will only make things worse, and you will train your mind to lie awake in bed. If you can't fall asleep after fifteen or twenty minutes, then get out of bed and do something else for an hour. When I can't sleep because something is bothering me, I get up and write down what I will do the next day to solve the problem. This helps me settle down and get back to sleep.

- **When you go to bed, try some controlled-breathing exercises or meditation techniques.** Inhale deeply and exhale deeply ten times. Then mediate for five to ten minutes. This helps me settle down if I've had a busy or stressful day.

- **Don't eat or drink late at night before going to bed.** I don't eat after dinner anymore. I find that if I eat late at night, I have trouble falling and staying asleep. Eating a healthy diet will also help you sleep better. Foods that are high in fat, dairy, caffeine, and inflammatory ingredients are going to keep you up at night. You don't want to go to bed at night with a bloated stomach because you just ate a large pizza.

- **Make sure you invest in a first-rate mattress and a therapeutic pillow.** With mattresses, you get what you pay for, so don't skimp on these items. Again, sleeping well has a huge impact on how well you're able to change your life. I've realized how quality sleep has helped me succeed and changed my life in so many ways. That's why sleep has now become one of my biggest priorities—it has set me on the path to success.

If you truly aren't sleeping well, I recommend that you see your doctor to make sure you aren't suffering from a medical condition that is affecting your sleep. You could also try reading one or more of the many good books on the market that help you understand and plan for quality sleep. We will talk about diet, exercise, and stress later in this chapter. These are all factors in promoting good sleep.

Food

I used to live my life eating junk food that was inflammatory to my body. Now, I live it eating healthy food. The difference in the way I have felt during these two phases of my life is extraordinary. Eating quality food is like putting high-octane gasoline in a race car. Changing your life and becoming rich is like running a competitive race. If you want your race car to excel and win the race, you'd better take care of it. You need to give it top-quality fuel. Food is your fuel for success. Unhealthful food brings about an inferior performance, while healthful food will allow you to give your peak performance. It's that simple. If you want to change your life and become rich, you need to eat healthy food.

Consider the story I presented at the beginning of this chapter. My health was suffering so much that I thought about giving up playing competitive sports for good. One day I was playing tennis with a friend, and, after ten minutes, I was on one knee, trying to catch my breath. My friend told me I really needed to go see a doctor. I took his advice and went to see a cardiologist for a complete stress test. The verdict: There was nothing medically wrong with me.

A few days later, I heard about a recently published book that detailed the types of food that cause inflammation in the body. I realized my entire diet was made of these inflammatory foods: dairy, gluten, processed sugar, sodium, processed meat, and other processed foods. My diet consisted of a loaf of bread every two days, four daily pints of milk, and ice cream and cookies every evening. Most of my lunches and dinners were made up of pasta, gnocchi, and pierogies. During my driving for work, I'd stop by the convenience store or a coffee shop for flavored mochas and pastries. I also met clients and vendors for breakfast several times a week, where I would consume bacon, sausage, or ham. Almost everything I was consuming had some form of dairy, gluten, processed sugar, sodium, or processed meat in it. I was a walking body of inflammation.

I decided to try to avoid inflammatory foods and see if it helped me feel better. I switched from dairy milk to almond or coconut milk. I went from eating ice cream every night to only once a week. I gave up the stops at convenience stores for sugary coffees and snacks. I gave up cookies. I switched to rice-based pasta and gluten-free bread products. I limited my bacon consumption to once every two weeks. I tried not to give up everything I loved—I was just striving for more moderation. Let's be real here: I am not going to live without bacon and ice cream!

The new diet significantly changed my health. Within four short weeks of changing my eating habits, all the conditions from which I was suffering disappeared. I couldn't believe it! The pain in my feet, elbow, wrist, and shoulder were completely gone. I was able to work twelve-hour days without feeling tired. I could play five sets of tennis without getting winded or overheated. It has been four years since I made the changes to my diet, and I have never felt better in all my life. I haven't had a single relapse in any of my past conditions or ailments. They seem to be permanently gone. I know this sounds hard to believe. When I tell people this story, they look at me with disbelief—but it's true.

There are dozens of books on healthy eating and anti-inflammatory diets. Magazine and blog articles abound that cover healthful eating. Start to make healthful eating—and learning about healthful eating—a regular part of your life. You will feel better, have a positive attitude, sleep better, and increase your motivation to succeed. If you want to change your life and become rich, you must improve your diet. You need both your mind and body to support your success and goals.

Water

Staying properly hydrated is an essential part of maintaining a healthy body and keeping your brain at optimum performance. Your brain is like the engine in a race car. If the engine is rusty or overheating, then the car breaks down, and the driver can't finish the race. Water to your brain is like oil to a car. Our brains are 83 percent water. Brains that aren't hydrated won't operate at peak performance. Our brains drive our motivation, happiness level, and focus.

Research has shown that drinking water upon waking has many health benefits, such as improved digestion, better complexion, and reduced wrinkles. People have also found that they have better energy throughout the day, reduced symptoms from diseases, and an easier time with weight loss. I have found that the habit not only flushes the toxins from your body but also promotes your immune system and just generally makes you happier.

When I started to focus on drinking water in the morning and throughout the day, my remaining ulcerative-colitis symptoms disappeared. Also, my tennis game improved. Back when I adopted an anti-inflammatory diet to improve my physical stamina on the tennis court, I also started to focus on my level of hydration. Much of my lack of stamina was due to a poor diet, but it was also due to being dehydrated. These days, I always make sure I show up to the tennis court with plenty of water in my system and extra water to drink while I am playing. My on-court stamina improved dramatically when I began to drink plenty of water during the hours leading up to a tennis match.

Numerous professional athletes start their day by consuming water on an empty stomach before they do anything else. I can honestly say I feel more awake and vibrant when I start my day with a pint of filtered water.

If you drink at least eight to ten glasses of water every day, it flushes all the toxins and helps your body to function properly. A well-known health regimen involving water is Japanese water therapy, which helps to clean your stomach and boost your digestive system. Japanese traditional medicine recommends drinking water right after waking up in the morning. It is believed that drinking water on an empty stomach when you first wake up not only promotes weight loss by smoothing out your digestive system but also helps in treating various health problems. Japanese water therapy helps relieve stress, promotes weight loss, and ensures a strong digestive system. Most of all, it keeps you energetic throughout the day. Drinking enough water during the day also revs up your metabolism.

If you want to try Japanese water therapy, drink about twenty ounces of water when you first wake up, even before you brush your teeth. The water should be at room temperature—not chilled. Try to abstain from eating or drinking anything else for forty-five minutes after the water, and then have your breakfast. Also, a part of this practice is to avoid eating or drinking anything for about two hours after every meal of the day. Of course, if you have an issue that prevents you from drinking that much water at one time, you can drink what you can and try to gradually increase it to twenty ounces eventually.

Exercise

If I had a dime for every article, study, or news show talking about how exercise promotes longevity and reduces disease and stress, I would be rich from that alone. I have played sports and worked out most of my life, except for a couple of periods when I was less active. I spent the first ten years after I graduated from college without a habit of exercise and then again when I was going through that bad breakup and business divorce. During these periods, I also experienced the worst health of my life. I looked unhealthy, felt terrible, and had numerous health problems. My friends and family often told me I looked sick. My stomach problems were so bad that I was hospitalized for five days. I had joint problems and was tired all the time.

During the more-active periods of my life, my near-perfect health has enabled me to accomplish my educational, business, and financial goals. Right now, I'm playing tennis three times a week. I have no health problems, and people tell me I look great.

The many benefits of exercise include:

- Healthy digestive system
- Healthy weight
- An increase in bone density

- An increase in muscle mass
- Good sleep
- Lack of stress
- A better appearance
- Improved sex drive
- Better-looking skin
- Help with conditions like heart disease and diabetes
- A healthy brain
- Boost in confidence and self-esteem
- Healthier joints and reduced back problems
- Improved circulation

I am confident that if you include regular exercise in your life, you will greatly improve your chances of changing your life and reaching a point of personal and financial freedom. Studies show that the human body is made for movement. Exercise and movement promote good health, and good health gives us the platform for building wealth as we would like.

Avoid Stress and Toxic People

Stress can derail you from accomplishing your goals, cause major health problems, and even kill you. From personal experience, I know what it can do to a person if it goes unchecked. If you want to change your life, build wealth, and reach your goals, then you must be able to identify stress, eliminate it, or counteract its effects on you.

Stress can be caused by a number of factors. Sometimes the factors are obvious, but other times, it takes some self-reflection to find them. Think about how these examples of stress might be influencing you at the moment:

- Aggravating boss or co-workers
- Bad finances
- Toxic people in your life
- Watching and listening to negative media
- Health problems experienced by you or your loved ones
- Abusive life partners, siblings, or parents
- Bad diet
- Lack of exercise
- Putting poisons into your body

Handling stress is like all the other subjects in this book. The solution is not one thing alone but rather meshes with all aspects of your lifestyle. If you read and implement the knowledge in the chapters on developing your mindset, surrounding yourself with the right people, guarding your time, or becoming financially responsible, then you are essentially reading about how to remove stress from your life. Some proven ways to reduce stress are listed below. You will notice that many connect to other areas of health or your other Life Assets.

- Find role models and positive people to be around
- Get abusive people out of your life

- Change jobs if you aren't happy
- Eat a healthful diet
- Stop watching violent or negative TV
- Get off social media if you use it just for entertainment
- Get regular exercise
- Get out of debt, and start saving money
- Stay hydrated
- Get eight hours of sleep

The way you take care of your body will ultimately help you better achieve your goals of becoming successful. If you think of your body as a tool that needs quality sleep, a proper diet, daily hydration, and regular exercise, you'll feel good, look good, and be able to rise to any height you desire. However, if you don't take care of yourself, you'll drop into an abyss of defeat.

I want you to have a great life, full of opportunity and growth. The bottom line is this: if you want to accomplish your goals, your mind and body must be in peak condition. It doesn't matter if you are an athlete, student, or entrepreneur—you *must* have good health to succeed in any area of life.

Putting It Together

We all know that good health makes pursuing all our other wealth-building goals easier. Developing your Life Asset #1: Mindset goes a long way toward strengthening and developing your mental health. Mental and physical health go hand in hand, so learn from my challenges with my own health to avoid those challenges for yourself. Build health resilience by getting good-quality sleep, filling your body with sustaining foods, increasing your water intake, and developing new exercise routines in your life. Your current and future self will thank you for leveraging your Life Asset #6: Health, and you will be reaching your goals sooner than you imagined.

Strategies to Develop Your Life Asset #6: Health

In this chapter, you discovered a multitude of examples and helpful suggestions aimed at helping you develop Life Asset #6: Health. Below, you'll find practical steps to jump-start your journey right now:

5 quick things to do right now:

1. Set up your bedroom to be more favorable for sleep.
2. Replace one food/drink you know is not building good health with something that will.
3. Increase your water intake, even if it is just one glass a day.
4. Decide on an individual or group sport (or just think "movement") that you can add to your week.
5. Go out of your way to communicate with one person who you already know improves your mood or reduces stress for you.

Extra Credit: Research and read a book about health that challenges you to form a new health-related habit.

◆ ◆ ◆

FINAL THOUGHTS

Whatever you spend a lot of time doing, that is what you will be good at. I spend all my time thinking and acting like a rich person and leveraging my six Life Assets. The result is that, every day, my net worth and income keep growing.

After I graduated from college with my degree in electrical engineering, I worked as an engineer outside of Boston at a semiconductor company. One of our tactics for competing with other semiconductor companies was to purchase their products, take the product apart, see how it worked, and then try to design a better version. This is a common practice today amongst competitors in all types of industries. Taking apart the competitor's product is known as reverse engineering. Redesigning a better version of the product is known as re-engineering.

This book is about reverse engineering your life and re-engineering a version that will empower you to obtain everything you desire. If you want to change and become rich, then you must deconstruct your life and reconstruct the life of a person who thinks and acts like someone who is personally and financially free. If you do this, you will build wealth in multiple ways and be able to use your time as *you* choose.

You must change what you do with your six Life Assets. These truly are superpowers if you use them wisely. You must change what you eat, drink, watch, and listen to. You might have to change jobs or careers along the way. You will almost certainly have to change who you trust and spend time with. Changing what you do with your time and money will be necessary on your new journey.

I promise you that, if you take this journey, every aspect of your life will improve. Being in control of your emotions, health, happiness, and financial situation is an incredible feeling. I love getting out of bed every day and spending my day creating abundance, prosperity, and wealth, and sharing it with people like you. It is a great feeling to realize that nothing in life is about fate or luck. We are in complete control of how we live our lives and what life brings to us. Go forward working smart and hard to bring value to other people, and you will be rewarded for the rest of your life.

In the chapters that preceded this conclusion, we've journeyed together through my failures, my hard-learned lessons, and my growth. I had to hit rock bottom to fully grasp the significance of the Six Life Assets. You don't have to. My hope is that my story will serve as a cautionary tale, a lesson in what not to do, as well as an inspiring road map for what is possible when you shift your mindset and manage your Life Assets wisely.

Do I have it all figured out now? Of course not. This is a never-ending process of growth and adaptation. But I can tell you this: Since I started treating these areas of my life as assets, not only have I seen tangible improvements in my financial and professional world, but my relationships are stronger, my health is better, my mind is sharper, and, above all, my spirit is lighter. I've turned a page and found a life worth living, filled with purpose and joy.

So, what's next for you? You hold the pen. You are the author of your life. Take a long, hard look at your Six Life Assets. How are you managing them? Are the Assets truly serving you, or are they liabilities dragging you down? Ask yourself hard questions, confront uncomfortable truths,

FINAL THOUGHTS

and don't be afraid to make changes. Remember, the most significant investment you can ever make is in yourself.

With these words, I'm not ending a book; I'm opening a door—a door to a richer, more meaningful, more fulfilling life. All you've got to do is step through it.

You have the same God-given talent and potential as everyone else. You can become or do anything you want. You can obtain everything life has to offer. In today's world, there is more abundance, opportunity, and wealth than ever before, and there is no reason or excuse for you not to acquire your share of it. I wish you massive change, success, and happiness.

If your life is the same five years from now, will you be okay with that?

The time to change your life is right now!

♦ ♦ ♦

ABOUT THE AUTHOR

J*oseph Herbert* is a real estate investor, business entrepreneur, speaker, coach, writer, and content creator. He has owned bars, restaurants, and night clubs. He is the founder of the Joe Herbert Realty real estate brokerage in Erie, Pennsylvania and the SelfMadeWealth.co online wealth education company. He is a member of Rotary International and a past president of the Rotary Club of Erie. He graduated from Rochester Institute of Technology with a BS in electrical engineering and spent 25 years in the corporate world as an electrical engineer and software developer. His Job Free Economy podcast can is on Apple podcasts, iHeart, Stitcher, and Spotify.

SelfMadeWealth.co